Extinction is Forever
and other stories

'Be welcome, *homo sapien*,' Kermondley said.
'His name's Stephen,' said Vanya.
'And we were hardly wise,' Stephen admitted.
Kermondley smiled.
'It's a little late to realize that, my friend.'
'Not where I come from,' Stephen said.
'Space?' Kermondley asked hopefully.
'Time,' said Stephen. '2005.'
Kermondley nodded.
His fear was established now.

ALSO BY LOUISE LAWRENCE

EXTINCTION IS FOREVER
and other stories

LOUISE LAWRENCE

RED FOX

A Red Fox Book

Published by Random Century Children's Books
20 Vauxhall Bridge Road, London SW1V 2SA

A division of the Random Century Group

London Melbourne Sydney Auckland
Johannesburg and agencies throughout the world

First published by The Bodley Head Children's Books 1990

Red Fox edition 1991

'Extinction is Forever' and 'Rigel Light' first
appeared in *Out of Time* (Bodley Head, 1984), and
'The Silver Box' in *A Quiver of Ghosts* (Bodley
Head, 1987).

Printed and bound in Great Britain by
Cox & Wyman Ltd, Reading, Berkshire

ISBN 0 09 985060 5

Contents

1

The Inheritors

Cilla breathed deeply. And they sat on floor cushions around her, their hands linked, their eyes closed, their minds emptied of thought. Soon she would go into trance and Oris would speak.

'Is there anybody there?' said Alan.

Elaine waited. Unwanted thoughts flittered through her head and she could not be rid of her awareness . . . of the hands holding hers and the itch on her leg which she wanted to scratch. The room was cold . . . the fire unlit . . . and wind whined down the chimney. Tendrils of ivy tapped like fingers on the window pane and distracted her.

'Is there anybody there?' repeated Alan.

Elaine opened her eyes.

It was 2021, a grey February dawn. The mountains were dark on the far horizon, apple-blossom pale and ghostly in the orchard where the community caravans were parked. Bryndur had grown since she came there ten years ago. She tried to remember it as it had been . . . a derelict hill farm at the head of a bleak Welsh valley, its fields choked with bracken and gorse and the house unfit for habitation. She had been a young child then, living with Alan and Patti, her father and mother, in a single caravan . . . squatters reclaiming the land. They had survived on goats' milk and a crop of potatoes . . . until Cilla arrived.

Cilla came from Birmingham. She had been Patti's friend at university, a psychic medium in touch with

7

unseen realms of existence, and Oris was her guide. He claimed to be a higher spirit from another part of the galaxy, an invisible being who taught them how to live in harmony with each other and the land. Under Oris's guidance Bryndur thrived. Now there were a dozen families living and working there. They grew acres of wheat and organic vegetables, kept sheep on the mountains and made their own clothes, a self-sufficient community except for things like soap and salt. Self-sufficient, thought Elaine, yet they were totally dependent on Cilla and Oris . . . every man, woman and child, required to trust and obey.

'Is there anybody there?'

It was how they began the day — each day and every day — sitting in a circle around Cilla. Each day they received instructions, listened to advice, asked questions, gained answers, debated what they had heard and then carried it out. It was the content of the messages that mattered, said Alan, not whether Oris was real or not.

Elaine shivered. Her breath made smoke and she had never known it be so cold before. Almost, she thought, it was cold enough to freeze. Or maybe snow? And if it did . . . how would they cope? They had no fuel for heating, just peat for the cooking stove in the kitchen and a dozen uninsulated caravans. She supposed Oris would tell them.

'Oris?' whispered Patti. 'Are you there?'

'Greetings, children of Earth,' said Cilla.

But the voice was not hers.

It was deeper and more manly.

Elaine stared at her. She was plump and fortyish, wore flowing patchwork robes and flowing hair, bracelets and earrings that jangled when she walked. Cilla had things easy, Elaine thought sourly. Unlike the rest of them she seldom dirtied her hands. She was simply there, available with Oris for personal consultations, queen of the commune and ruling them all. And the voice that was not Cilla's went on.

8

'I am Oris from the fifth dimension of space and time. We, of the Astral, from the Brotherhood of the planet Og, salute you.'

'We're glad you could make it,' said Alan.

'It is my duty to attend your meetings,' said Oris. 'And it is my mission to instruct and teach you. You are souls, just as we are, although not so advanced. Your memory is lost, your vision clouded by reincarnation. Existence on the physical level is never easy. Yet you are connected to all that is. The power that flows through the universe, through stones and stars and every living thing, is manifest in you.'

Elaine sighed.

She had heard it all before, everything reiterated and reiterated. It was actually boring . . . long droning monologues on the shortcomings of mankind, exposés of all their human failings and how to overcome them . . . how to raise their individual vibrations and realize their individual potentials . . . how to desire and not desire, to care and not to care. Then came the minutiae of daily living . . . what to eat and what to think on . . . where and when and what to plant and how to nurture it . . . the need to respect the planet and each other. No mention of the weather though. It seemed that the lesson for today was a directive on sharing the knowledge they had gained at Bryndur and teaching others how to live.

'Responsibility belongs to the individual,' said Oris. 'What you have done here must be done elsewhere. You all know the situation. The Earth is sick and there is global chaos due to the climatic changes. No person, no nation, is untouched by the destruction of the last century. The environment is damaged, but it is not beyond repair. Now is the time for rebuilding and that is your task. You, and others like you, must usher in the New Age . . . an age based, not on selfishness and self-interest, but on love and sharing.'

Elaine sniffed.

The cold was making her nose run and what Oris said

was all very well, but the people of Llangoed were hardly likely to listen. For what had happened to the British economy, to society in general and to the world, they blamed the government. And they believed the ones who lived at Bryndur were a bunch of English weirdos, religious fanatics and long-haired freaks.

Elaine gazed at them . . . Alan, her father, with his multi-coloured trousers and bristling beard . . . Patti, her mother, red-haired and freckled with jasmine in her hair . . . bald-headed Nick who had LOVE tattooed on his forehead . . . Pru and Deirdrie from Bristol Polytechnic, who spun and wove and knitted . . . Mike in his tattered sheepskin jerkin, his hair tied in a pigtail, who made medicines out of herbs. Maybe they *were* freaks, she thought, every one of them mad. They had to be mad to believe in Oris. The very idea of an invisible being from another planet talking to them through Cilla was insane.

'When it comes to teaching I foresee certain problems,' said Alan.

'To see them is to create them,' Oris replied.

'He's asking us to trust him,' said Patti.

'Like we always have,' said Pru.

But Elaine no longer trusted.

Nor did she believe.

Later, after breakfast in the communal kitchen where Cilla lingered at the table drinking dandelion coffee, where Elaine washed up for thirty-two people and Patti stoked the fire-oven ready for baking, Di Jones called. His was the next farm down the valley, almost as derelict as Bryndur had been. At seventy-five, alone since the death of his wife, he was too old to work it. But he still kept sheep on the mountain. And they should be brought down, now, this very day, said Di, for there would be snow before nightfall. He could smell it, feel it in his bones.

Elaine felt a small thrill.

How odd she should have thought about snow.

Maybe she had psychic abilities too?

But Cilla frowned.

'We don't have snow in England,' she announced.

'Not these days,' said Patti.

'This is Wales!' growled Di. 'And I am telling you! A spell of bad weather we are in for and them sheep will be likely to die in the drifts if they are not brought down.'

He knew, thought Elaine. He actually knew. It was an instinct inside him, an absolute certainty. Dogs sat at his heels, their yellow eyes gleaming, and a chill wind blew through the open doorway. It was something to do with trusting yourself, Elaine thought. And the men were away at the slag heap sifting for coal.

'There's no one here except us,' Patti said worriedly.

'And Oris said nothing about snow,' said Cilla.

'Maybe Oris doesn't know everything,' Elaine suggested.

'He would have advised us!' Cilla retorted.

'He's not God, is he?'

'Perhaps you should consult him?' Patti said quickly.

'I am not waiting here all day!' grumbled Di. 'Either you are coming with me to fetch them sheep, or you are not . . . but I am not waiting.'

Elaine wiped her hands on the rag of a towel.

'I'll fetch my coat,' she said.

'*You* can't go up Pen Ivan!' said Patti.

'I can open gates and help with the droving.'

'If it's truly going to snow it might be dangerous!'

'And what about your duties here?' asked Cilla. 'You're supposed to be helping your mother with the baking!'

'You're not doing anything,' said Elaine. 'Why don't you help her?'

Cilla's eyes flashed angrily.

'We shall have to ask Oris about *her*,' she said to Patti.

In spite of Oris, Elaine made her decision. She swapped her knitted slipper-socks for a pair of hand-made moccasins, took a crude sheepskin jacket from the closet, wound a long knitted scarf around her neck and made to leave. When it came to sheep and mountains and weather conditions she knew who to trust. Di Jones had a lifetime of experience based on reality, unlike Oris who floated around in some astral plain where the white light always shone.

Closing the door quietly behind her Elaine followed him across the farmyard. The dogs frisked around the gatepost and cocked their legs, and free range chickens fled squawking from their path. Goats stamped restlessly in the byre and milk buckets clanked, and women churned cheeses in the dairy. Children chanted tables in an upstairs schoolroom in the house. But the sounds of the community faded as they headed up the track between walled fields. Peas, beans, sweetcorn and potatoes, sprouted in green rows among a fresh mulch of manure.

Di wiped his nose on his sleeve.

And sniffed revoltingly.

'You can't grow that kind of stuff up here,' he said.

'*We* do,' said Elaine.

'It is not natural.'

'There are some communities who grow crops in pure sand,' Elaine informed him. 'And all we use is compost and caring.'

'And all that mumbo-jumbo and hocus-pocus,' Di said darkly.

'You don't like us, do you?'

'I've got no time for it, see?'

He whistled the dogs.

He was old and crabby, smelling worse than the manure of body odour and unwashed clothes. Elaine walked ahead of him, on up the track. There, where the fields ended, the hills opened out and she felt suddenly free. Clean and cold, the wind whistled down the scree slopes and cotton-grass fluttered in white masses among miles of bog and rushes and brown dead heather. Clumps of pink flowering saxifrage shivered among the stones. There was a power, Oris said, a power that flowed through the universe, through stones and stars and every living thing. It flowed through Elaine, strong and awesome and lonely, like love sweeping her away into crags and a curlew's cry and streams of tumbling water. It was all part of God, she thought. But then she turned to look back and the feeling fled.

It was always the same. Elaine could look at trees or flowers, a field of wheat or cabbages in rain, and see them as perfect creations, feel they were holy. But when it came to people her imagination failed. She could see nothing of God in Cilla ruling the commune, in Patti red-faced from the fire and meekly obedient, in Alan grown thin and exhausted from years of work. And nothing of God in Di Jones tramping up the track in a pair of worn-out boots, his clothes gone to rags, his trousers tied up with string . . . nor in the people of Llangoed with their grievances and jealousies. Somehow, she thought, the spirit that flowed through all things detoured around people or else died on arrival. Unless there was a fault within herself? An inability to love?

Oris talked endlessly of love. They all talked of it. The whole community was based on it . . . the power of love, the spirit of love, love of each other and the earth. Everything they did had to be done with love, and everything they said had to be spoken with love in their hearts. Elaine understood the principle, yet more and more she began to resent it. She did not see it as love . . . she saw it as work, chores done by duty rota, eroding her freedom, her energy, her time. And they were not particularly loving at Bryndur; they were just people living together, irritating, intruding, demanding. At sixteen she was old enough to pull her weight, they had decided.

She stared down the valley to Llangoed, a grey town of grey terraced houses in a grey cold land. Grassed-over slag heaps rose behind it, and plantations of conifers growing on the mountains ringed it around. No love there either, thought Elaine. It was a bitter place, like the ending of the world, an old civilization dying. And no way out of it except by bus, once every week on Saturdays. Ramshackle red, she watched it rattling down the road to Cardiff. She wished she were on it, going with Pru and Deirdrie to sell their knitwear at the market. She wished she was anywhere except at Bryndur.

'Half-past nine,' she said when Di caught up with her.

'I dare say it is,' he wheezed.

'It's only taken us half an hour.'

'It will be taking us all day if you keep dilly-dallying.'

'I thought you might like a breather,' said Elaine.

'We've got no time for luxuries, girlie.'

'Not even five minutes?'

'No,' said Di. 'You look at them clouds.'

Elaine turned to face the mountains again.

The peak of Pen Ivan was lost in the murk.

And a single snowflake touched her.

It was unusually cold that February morning, cold such as Ewan had never known. Something was wrong with the Greenhouse effect, he thought. The sky above the housing estates looked leaden-grey and heavy, as if it would fall, and a sly wind rattled the hardboard in the broken bathroom window. There was no hot water. He washed in cold, searched the airing cupboard for an extra sweater, then went downstairs. Clumps of daffodils shivered among the tussocks of brown grass that had once been a lawn and convolvulus grew between the flagstones on the patio. Broken horizontal blinds hung skew-wiff across one of the glass doors and his parents were sitting in overcoats watching television. A half-empty jam pot and the remains of a loaf of bread waited on the table.

'What time d'you call this?' asked his father.

'Ten to eleven,' said Ewan.

'It's all right for some!'

'What's there to get up for?'

'It's slovenly staying in bed all day.'

'So what have you been doing?'

'Ssh!' said his mother. 'I want to watch.'

Ewan hated weekends. It was always the same. All they ever did was watch television, a day-long diet of nostalgia, of how things used to be . . . endless repeats of old series about the rich getting richer in an era which his parents remembered but Ewan did not. He had been born too late. Things were running down, running out . . . oil, gas, raw materials. And electricity was rationed to five units a day. A couple of hours heat and light, one cooked meal and a few litres of hot water, and that was the lot. Except that Ewan's parents used most of it for watching television.

He wanted to shake them, scream at them . . . it was all their fault! Their generation and the generation before them . . . millions and millions of comfortable people living their comfortable twentieth-century lives, not thinking about the future and not caring, but believing the good times would go on forever. The Smash-and-Grab Society, Ewan had called it in an essay written for history homework. Never mind the facts, the warnings . . . damage to the ozone layer and acid rain, the waste, the pollution, the felling of forests . . . they still went on wanting things, went on consuming. And their children inherited, Ewan inherited . . . a planet devastated and spent, rubbish dumps and closed-down factories, poisoned rivers and fished-out seas, sickly animals, soil erosion and defoliated trees.

And the house, of course. The house would be Ewan's one day . . . a nice little semi-detached on a select housing estate, built in the late 1980s and falling apart, ravaged by the storms of the 1990s. Large cracks zig-zagged down the living-room wall. The windows were rotting and woodlice nested behind the skirting boards. And the bread was stale, the toaster broken long ago.

He pushed away his plate.

'What's for lunch?' he demanded.

'Luncheon meat,' said his mother.

'Not again!'

'It's cheap and doesn't need cooking.'

'You could try turning off the telly and using the oven instead!'

'If you don't like it . . .' began his father.

'Ssh!' said his mother. 'I want to watch.'

Fast cars flashed across the screen, things of the past. Now, except for the doctor's and district nurse's, they rusted in scrap yards, taxed off the roads and with no petrol to run them. Ewan would never know how it felt to drive or possess one. Travel for him was a ride to Cardiff on a clapped-out bus, or a day-trip to Barry Island on a restored steam train, those parts of it that were not under water. Make-do-and-mend, was the present government's policy. But spare parts were hard to come by. Houses heaved with defunct appliances, although they kept the televisions going. Without television, the history teacher reckoned, there would likely be mass revolution. People actually needed it. People like Ewan's parents watched it and dreamed that the 'Dallas' days would come again, that there would be economic revival, industrial expansion, money and jobs. They did not want to face the truth that the old ways were over, Western civilization was in a state of collapse and hardship was here to stay.

But Ewan had no choice. He would be leaving school shortly and the future had nothing to offer him. This was the South Wales scrap heap. The steelworks was closed, coal-mines worked out, shops boarded up, businesses bankrupt, and unemployment was running at fifty per cent. If he were lucky he might labour for a pittance for a building firm renovating slum dwellings and demolishing others, repairing and reclaiming. Or, if he were even more lucky, he might work in a council hostel caring for people less fortunate than himself . . . the ill and the old and the dying, those who had dropped out or given up.

16

And that was no different from staying at home, he thought angrily. Wages for work and a Social Security allowance were more or less the same, and his parents had given up long ago.

He stared at them morosely, bitterly, from across the room. They were not that old, forty-five and fifty, but they might have been a hundred, two people more dead than alive. At some point in their lives they had stopped caring, Ewan decided, stopped in their minds and ceased to be aware. He tried to imagine them once upon a time, young and enthusiastic, conceiving a future for themselves and conceiving him, in touch with something real and possible. But all he could see was them now, apathetic and spiritless, clinging to their obsolete ideas, believing the lies of a government that promised Britain would be great again some day. Huddled in shabby coats at separate ends of the sofa, they fixed their attention on the television and did not want to know about him or anything else.

And the heatless house decayed around them.

And the world outside offered no hope.

Ewan stood up.

He would end up like them if he stayed.

'I'm going,' he said.

'Clear the table first,' said his father.

'I mean I'm going for good!'

'And mind you shut the door.'

'There's got to be more than this! There's got to be!'

'There's the News in five minutes. They might up the meat ration or the sugar ration.'

'You're not listening to me, are you?'

'Ssh!' said his mother. 'I want to watch.'

Ewan had no destination in mind. He caught a bus to Cardiff and another going up the valleys to Llangoed and Aberglas. It was half-past one when it left the depot. Hard rain splattered the windows and women queued outside the shops. Most things were rationed these days

. . . food and clothes and fuel . . . an imposed sharing. Not natural, thought Ewan, not people acting freely and sharing what there was because it was the right thing to do. It has to be enforced by coupons and rubber stamps and government law. And the young, in groups, roamed aimlessly through the streets not having any purpose. He wondered if it would be different in a smaller community, in Aberglas or Llangoed, or wherever he was going.

He glanced at the passengers — women with shopping bags mostly, come from the Saturday market, and two girls in tapestry coats nursing wicker baskets. Craft-hawkers, thought Ewan, who lived by selling what they made. It was one way of surviving if a person had talent. Briefly he admired them . . . their scrubbed clean looks, their bold bright clothes and animated conversation. They were both incomers, English by their accents, and possessed a kind of *joie de vivre*, a vivacity that was rare in that part of Wales. The women, in comparison, looked colourless and dowdy, their voices and faces dull and expressionless, as if they were shell-shocked after a war and the world in ruins around them. And it was, thought Ewan, the world they had known. The ruins of it were there outside, passing by the windows — crumbling estates of crumbling houses, rusting road signs, closed-down petrol stations and boarded-up fashion boutiques. Advertizing hoardings around a school playing field advised him not to have casual sexual relations or sit unprotected in the sun. And the rain seemed thicker, whiter, almost opaque, as if it were changing substance.

'It is turning to snow,' said the woman beside him.

'We don't have snow any more, not in this country,' said Ewan.

'I can remember when it used to snow regular, each winter.'

'That must have been years ago,' said Ewan.

'When I was a girl,' said the woman.

'The average temperature has risen by 1.75 degrees centigrade in the last twenty-five years,' Ewan informed her.

'Once, in Aberglas, we were cut off for more than a week,' said the woman.

'You live in Aberglas, do you?'

'Born there,' said the woman. 'But it is not like it was. I can remember, before the last pit closed . . .'

Here we go, thought Ewan.

It was always the same. People of her age could seldom talk of anything but the past. It was as if life stopped when they reached adulthood and the rest of it must be spent looking back and hankering. The present time, if they discussed it at all, was just something to grouse about, where everything got worse instead of better and where there were no positive changes. After sixteen years with his parents Ewan was sick of hearing about the twentieth century but, regardlessly, the woman reminisced. Her anecdotes were endless of how things used to be. And the windows steamed over as the bus rumbled on through an unseen land, stopping and starting and slowly emptying out.

'When I was your age we used to go disco-dancing,' said the woman. 'And there was pop-music playing in all the Cardiff shops. I can remember buying a fru-fru skirt when I was seventeen . . .'

Ewan stopped listening.

And the bus slowed down yet again. It had gone through Llangoed but Ewan decided he could not stick it all the way to Aberglas. Here was as good as anywhere, he thought, and across the gangway the two girls in tapestry coats rose to leave.

'Excuse me,' Ewan said.

'It was red,' said the woman. 'The latest fashion.'

'Excuse me! I want to get off!'

Flustered, the woman shifted her shopping bag and heaved to her feet. Ewan pushed past her. 'Fashion!' he thought savagely. 'As if it bloody matters!' And he followed the girls with their baskets, until the handle of his carrier broke. Underpants, socks, frayed shirts, toothpaste and soap, all his worldly possessions tipped on the floor among seats and feet. He had to scrabble to pick them up. And the unfolded items refused to fit.

'Hurry up!' the driver said impatiently.

The few remaining passengers watched and waited.

'You won't do it that way,' someone told him.

'Shall I help you fold it?' asked a woman.

'Oh sod it!' said Ewan.

He dumped his things on an empty seat.

And he left with nothing.

The shock hit him as the bus drove away. White, whirling, the snow was all about him, thick on the ground, filling the air. He had seen nothing like it, never in all his life. An experience of snow . . . he stood in total bewilderment watching the wheel tracks whiten on the road, feeling the cold flakes touch him and melt on his hands and face. A chill struck upwards through his shoes, canvas trainers worn to holes and already soaked. Slowly his toes turned numb. And the anorak bought last year at a jumble sale was not exactly weather-proof. He felt wetness soaking his back and realized the truth of his predicament.

Snow, driven by the wind, blinded and stung as he gazed around. There was nothing to see anyway . . . just miles and miles of emptiness, bracken and bog and outcrops of rock, dry-stone walls in a storm-racked land. He was stuck in a blizzard in the middle of nowhere and he was totally alone.

'You great steaming git!' Ewan told himself. 'Why the hell didn't you look before you got off the bus?'

But it was too late now.

And he could die of exposure if he did not soon find shelter.

'So what'll you do?' he demanded.

'Get moving,' he said.

'Which way though?' he wondered. 'Where's them girls?' They've got to live somewhere here-abouts.'

Uphill or down the road was empty, although it was hard to see through the white snow whirling. It dissolved the shapes of things and if anything moved it was instantly lost. Ewan had nothing to go on, only a vague memory of Llangoed that might be miles down the valley and an instinct inside him that said he ought to go up. It was almost like a voice guiding him. There was a farm up there, it said. Ewan obeyed and five minutes later, on the edge of a track, he saw the faint traces of footsteps.

Elaine's moccasins were cold and sodden, her feet gone numb. And the snow covered her, clung to her clothes and her hair. The mountains were growing dangerous, visibility reduced to a few metres ahead. Twice Di lost his footing, slipped on the scree slopes and fell. He was not hurt, but he was shaken, and they had to wait for him to recover. Anxiety gnawed at Elaine's stomach. For some reason she felt responsible for him . . . and the cold ate into her, stiffening her limbs . . . and he was an old man, less resilient than she. His breathing rattled and their progress was slow as he picked his way, warily, between the rocks. She stayed close to him, fearing he might fall again, no longer caring how much he smelt.

'I am not so spry as I was,' admitted Di.

'I'll look out for you,' Elaine assured him.

'Old is a liability, see?'

'Why?' asked Elaine.

'No use to anyone, are we?'

'You *know* things,' said Elaine.

'But we are not wanted,' said Di.

'You can always come and live at Bryndur. We don't turn anyone away.'

Di sniffed.

'First we are having to get there,' he muttered.

Elaine had no idea where they were. The snow changed everything and she had lost all sense of direction. But Di seemed to know and she had no choice but to trust him . . . his memory, his instinct, his knowledge-of-a-lifetime which she lacked. And the dogs had vanished long ago, gone before them, driving the sheep to the valley.

'How much further?' asked Elaine.

'Down here,' muttered Di.

She went on following him single-file among the rocks and stones, until a darkness loomed through the whirling snow and the crags rose to one side. They were sheltered then, the path going clear and level beneath an overhanging cliff before it dropped steeply downwards again to skirt the corrie lake beneath. Recognizing where she was Elaine felt suddenly relieved. Black water glittered and there was only one more slope before the mountains gentled and walking became easier down the last mile of track.

Then, as she stepped from the lee of the cliff, the wind hit her, struck like a fist, pummelling down the scree slopes of Pen Ivan. Di tottered. Old and powerless he went where it blew him, grabbed her scarf and slithered over the sheer edge, half-strangling her as she tried to hold on. There was nothing she could do to save him. Wedged between the rocks, she could only cling to ease the tension around her neck, taking the strain as the scarf stretched. She thought, for a moment, that her arms would be pulled from her sockets, until Di landed.

He was balanced on a ledge a little way beneath her. She took a chance, unwound the scarf from her neck. And his voice was a scream.

'Don't let go, girlie!'

'I won't!' gasped Elaine.

'I'll fall if you let go!'

'Don't worry . . . I'll hang on.'

Snow and her own hair whirled about her.

'I'll try pulling you up!' she shouted.

'Just give me a minute,' panted Di.

'You're all right, are you?'

'I have hurt my shoulder, see?'

Elaine waited.

And the scarf tensed as Di found a foothold.

'Try now!' he shouted.

Leaning back into the wind Elaine braced her feet against the stones . . . and pulled. Her arms ached and trembled with the strain and the scarf cut fiercely at the palms of her hands. And Di was a dead weight on the end of it, an old man lacking agility, unable to heave himself up. Desperately she tried again. Hot sweat soaked her and the effort made her feel sick.

'I can't do it!' she cried.

'Don't you let go!' Di said urgently.

'Oh God,' groaned Elaine. 'What'll we do?'

'I am needing a hand,' said Di.

It was a statement of fact. As he balanced on the ledge again the strain eased, enough for Elaine to flex her fingers and pull the scarf tight around a jutting spur of rock. But he still clung to it, dependent for his life, and she could not let go. They were stuck there, both of them, with no one to help. And the afternoon darkened . . . and the mountains were invisible through the blinding snow . . . and the wind snatched away Elaine's voice, stupidly crying 'Help me! Help me!' in a land where no one was.

They were going to die, she thought.

'Do not let go!' Di called feebly.

'I won't,' said Elaine.

But she knew she could not hold on forever. Her hands and feet were already numb, raw pain gone to unfeelingness. In the wind the tears on her face had turned to ice, her lips were frozen and she was too cold to shiver. Then quite suddenly, it ceased to matter. She could do nothing about it so what was the point of being afraid? And her fear dissolved, instantly with her thought, and a strange floating calm took hold of her mind. The snow was almost warm as it touched her. She closed her eyes and began to pray.

'Help me, Oris!'

She did not believe in him, yet she had to believe. Her

trust in him was the only hope she had. If he existed, if he was real, he would know what had happened and where she was. He would go to Cilla, send her a vision, relay instructions, and she would inform the men. Perhaps they were already on their way . . . Alan and Nick and the others, bringing ropes and blankets and physical strength, with Oris to guide them, a disembodied being from another world. Elaine had only to wait. And the waiting seemed almost pleasant. Her senses drifted, gone beyond pain, no longer aware of anything, no longer caring.

Then there was a shout in her head.

She was jolted awake.

And the strain was in her arms.

And her muscles ached.

'Are you all right?' she called to Di.

But he gave no answer.

He had probably died of the cold, thought Elaine.

And she screamed in panic.

'Someone, please help!'

Impossible to see where he was going. Snow, driven by the wind, blew in Ewan's face and he bent his head. And the track went upwards with stone walls on either side and a gate at the top which he assumed led into a farmyard . . . until he opened it and blundered into a flock of sheep. They must have been waiting there, patiently, their dirty grey fleeces heavy with snow. No chance of stopping them. They milled around him and past him, piled through the gateway and headed down the way he had come. And behind them came the dogs, a pair of Welsh Collies with bright yellow eyes who regarded him briefly, quizzically, and then vanished silently after the sheep. But where there were sheep and dogs, Ewan reasoned, there should be a shepherd. So he waited . . . but no one came.

'Odd,' said Ewan.

He called and listened.

The wind and snow froze him.

And still no one came.

'Something's wrong,' he concluded.

'Something is wrong,' echoed the voice in his head.

'So what'll I do?'

'You know what to do,' said the voice in his head.

'Find them,' said Ewan.

'Find them,' confirmed the voice in his head.

All Ewan really wanted to do was find the farm. But there was some other occupant inside his skull, forcing him to move, willing him on up the track. He was mad, he thought, suffering from hypothermia and mentally deranged. Cold in his feet made a pain. His face ached and his hands were numb. And there were mountains ahead, dangerous for a person who did not know them. Yet, somehow, it seemed he *did* know them, or else he was being informed. Rocks, snow-drifts, bogs and sheer edges, he managed to avoid them all, as if someone guided him or some strange instinct kept him on the path. Snow-blinded, wind battered, cold and exhausted, Ewan continued to battle his way upwards.

'This is stupid!' he groaned.

'You must go on,' said the voice in his head.

'Important, is it?'

'Human lives are always important.'

'How do I know that I'm not making you up?'

Then Ewan heard a cry that was not in his head.

Nearby was a lake of black water, but she was a girl calling for help among the unseen ridges beyond. Desperately, urgently, she called. 'Which way do I go?' asked Ewan. But his mind was a blank. The voice in his head had abandoned him and there was no one to guide him but the girl herself.

'Help me! Help me! Someone, please help!'

Ewan cupped his hands.

'I'm coming, girlie! Where are you?'

After that he forgot the wind and weather and his own fatigue. Impelled by her need he tried to run. But the ground turned soggy. He sank to his knees in snow and bog, floundered among rushes and hauled his way out, making slow progress. And all the while the girl urged him to hurry, screamed in the wind. And the snow was in his face again as he scrambled up the slope towards her, slipping, sliding, clawing at the rocks. His legs ached horribly. Minutes seemed interminable and he thought he would never reach the top.

'Hurry! Please hurry!' cried the girl.

'Hang on . . . I'm almost with you.'

'I can't hang on much longer!'

'Just a few more minutes, girlie.'

'Can you see him yet?'

'See who?' shouted Ewan.

'On the ledge!' shouted the girl.

Briefly, above him, he glimpsed a tear-stained face and a flurry of long red hair among the snow, before he looked where she told him. And there, on the ledge, was an old man clinging to the lifeline of her scarf, a sheer drop beneath him. 'Bloody Hell!' muttered Ewan. But he did not have time to think. Crab-like he crawled sideways across the boulders. It was not that difficult . . . just a leap and a scramble was all it needed . . . easy for someone young.

'Grandad?' said Ewan.

The old man turned his head.

'Let's be having you, Grandad.'

Blue faded eyes stared into Ewan's own.

And he saw the old man's terror.

'Afraid you won't make it, are you?'

'I got no spring,' the old man whimpered. 'Rheumatics, see? And my fingers be too perished to grip.'

'I'll give you a hand,' said Ewan.

'Hurry up!' urged the girl.

'Don't you let go!' the old man wailed.

'She won't,' said Ewan. 'Now give us your hand.'

He lay on a rock, tucked his feet securely beneath it and leaned sideways over the edge. He was just able to reach. One frozen hand gripped his own. 'Now the other,' he instructed. The old man tottered, but Ewan stayed calm, poised and waiting as he released his hold on the scarf. Just for a few split seconds Ewan felt it . . . pain seering through his legs, a jolt on his arm, the heavy weight of a life that was not his own. Then he grabbed the free flailing hand and pulled. Steel-capped boots scraped on the stones, slipped and scrabbled as Ewan hauled him upwards on to solid ground.

'You all right, Grandad?'

The old man rolled over and sat up.

'I'm all right now,' he muttered.

'Ever thought of taking up absailing?' Ewan asked him.

Behind him someone laughed.

And he turned his head.

Beautiful, she was, in the gathering darkness among the wind and snow and mountains . . . a girl of his own age with green eyes and red hair. Rich and wild her laughter . . . until it turned hysterical. Then she was weeping, crying, sobs shaking her body . . . and he stared at her helplessly, not knowing what to say. Then, sharp and commanding, the voice returned to his head. Now was not the time or the place for human emotion, it said. If they were to survive they had to reach the farm before nightfall and they should move immediately.

'Quite right,' said Ewan. 'On your feet, Grandad. Best one forward . . . and you, girlie.'

Chit-chat seemed inappropriate out there on the mountains, apart from an exchange of names. How Ewan had come to find them was a long story and best left to another time, so they walked in silence with the wind at their backs and their arms linked and Di in between them. Anti-climactical, thought Ewan, and the constant falling of the snow was almost hypnotic. No sound but the wind and their breathing and the trudge of their footsteps, and the movement in the air going on and on. After a while his mind began to drift. He saw a glow of light in the gloom ahead, a shimmering whiteness that grew brighter as he walked towards it. And standing at the heart of it was a being in white robes. He was tall and insubstantial, the snow whirling behind his eyes, his voice a whisper in Ewan's head. From the fifth dimension of space and time he had come to advise him, he said.

'Alan!' shrieked Elaine.

'You see him too, do you?'

'Better late than never,' muttered Di.

The vision fled.

Ewan heard human voices calling.

He saw the lights of lanterns in the distances ahead.

'We're here! We're here!' shrieked Elaine.

Suddenly it was all over. When the men reached them Ewan was redundant, relieved of his responsibility, his life gone purposeless again. His connections were broken with Di and Elaine and he was just a stranger among strangers, obliged to explain himself. He was not local from Llangoed but had come that afternoon on the bus from Cardiff and got lost on the mountains.

'It was a miracle he found us,' said Elaine.

'Saved my life,' Di said gruffly. 'Him and the girlie.'

'So where were you going?' Alan asked him.

'Nowhere,' said Ewan. 'Nowhere in particular. Where is there to go? Anywhere or somewhere . . . it's all the same to me.'

'You mean you're homeless?'

'Sort of,' said Ewan. 'Right now in this moment I am.'

He did not have to ask.

The men accepted him, instantly, as if it was his right, and led him to the farm he had failed to find. Bryndur, it was called, and its kitchen was crowded with people, fluttering with candle-light and warm with fire. Confusion surrounded him, a peeling-off of wet clothes, women in bright dresses and long-haired men, concerned and ministering. They gave him dry socks, warm blankets to drape around his shoulders, home-made bread and soup in a pottery cup, sat him in a chair by the fire to steam and thaw.

'If you've nowhere to go you'd better stay here,' they said.

'Stay here with us.'

'You can sleep in the house tonight.'

'And later we'll find you a caravan.'

'We don't have a spare one at the moment.'

'But what's needed is sure to be provided.'

'It's the law of manifestation.'

'And it seldom fails.'

'All we have to do is trust.'

'I mean what would have happened out there on the mountains?'

'What would have happened if you hadn't arrived?'

'It was coincidence,' said Ewan.

'There's no such thing,' they told him.

'Everything's meant.'

'And you must have been sent for a purpose.'

Almost Ewan was tempted to tell them of the voice in his head but their attentions turned to Di the shepherd . . . how to prevent frostbite and pneumonia, what they had done with his sheep, and why it might be best if he stayed at Bryndur for the next few days. Or even permanently, suggested Alan. They could expand the community then, farm Di's land, and he in his old age would be taken care of.

'Think it over,' they urged him.

'We shall be glad to have you,' they said.

Snow tapped softly against the window and the night wind whined outside as Ewan listened and watched. They were strange people . . . the fat lady in flowing multi-coloured clothes . . . the bald-headed man with LOVE tattooed on his forehead . . . the girls he had seen on the bus . . . a red-haired woman with flowers in her hair who might be Elaine's mother . . . English, all of them, and full of strange ideas. All things happened for a purpose, they believe, and all life was sacred . . . stones and sheep and people sprung from the same source . . . and they were just caretakers here on Earth. Weirdos, thought Ewan, and nothing to do with him.

Suddenly he felt totally remote, as if they existed in a dream, their voices and faces gone far away in a world where he was not. Heat from the fire and his own tiredness set him adrift and his eyes felt leaden. Sleep sucked at his mind. The wind sang like music, and the room seemed to fade as he watched it, and a bright light was all around. Super-imposed on the white-washed walls and patchwork curtains Ewan saw a summer land of trees and flowers, as if there were two realities existing in the same space. And there, on the rag mat, clear as a ghost, stood the being in white robes.

'Greetings, Earth boy,' he said.

He must have been invisible and inaudible to everyone else for the fat woman with jangling earrings walked right through him.

'Who the hell *are* you?' Ewan asked.

'Cilla,' said the woman. 'And don't speak to me like that!'

'In my last incarnation,' said the being, 'I lived on the planet of Og.'

'Hog?' said Ewan. 'The planet of Hog?'

'What?' Cilla said sharply.

The room solidified and the ghost-shape faded.

And Cilla was staring at him with hostile eyes.

'What's that you said?'

'Hogs,' muttered Ewan. 'You keep hogs, do you?'

'No,' said Cilla haughtily. 'We're vegetarians. It helps raise our vibrations.'

'We are what we eat,' said one of the girls from the bus.

'There's nothing wrong with a nice bit of pork,' announced Di. 'If you can get it these days. And if I be staying here I shan't be living on no rabbit food.'

Elaine giggled and Cilla sniffed.

'I suppose we can't expect your kind to know any better.'

'My kind?' said Di. 'What's that then? You not of our species, missus?'

'Cilla's a New Age snob,' said Elaine.

Cilla turned on her furiously.

'How dare you!' she snapped.

Ewan stood up.

How they lived at Bryndur was nothing to do with him.

'I'll go to bed now, please,' he said loudly.

'Yes,' said Elaine. 'And so will I. And I shan't be coming to the morning meeting. I shan't be coming to it ever again.'

Elaine was determined . . . she was not going to be ruled by Cilla any longer. And most of what Oris said was obvious anyway, reiterations of the Buddah, Jesus Christ and Albert Einstein. It was not her fault that most of the human race had failed to listen, or twisted the meanings of all the sacred texts to meet their own ends. Nor was she responsible for the mess they had made of the Earth and all the ravages of the twentieth century. She only inherited the results and was obliged to make the best of it . . . and that did not mean spending the rest of her life churning cheeses in a remote Welsh valley, attending quasi-religious ceremonies and kow-towing to Cilla. She was not a child any longer. She was an adult . . . and an adult person should kowtow to no one, nor be subordinate.

Bitter feelings brewed at Bryndur that night after Ewan went to bed, and bitter in the morning when Elaine awoke. Patti and Alan refused to speak to her. They went as usual to the morning meeting and left her huddled beneath the bedclothes, damned for her declaration of independence. And so much for love, Elaine thought bitterly. You could only be loved if you did as you were told, conformed to other people's ideas of how you

31

should be. Oris had obviously failed dismally in his years of teaching. And the caravan was freezing. She had to breathe on the window to melt the ice.

Outside was a snowy landscape . . . stone walls buried in drifts, mountains pink with sunrise and apple trees iced with white. Everything dazzled, beautiful and intimidating, and a few small flakes of snow were still falling. It could snow for weeks, thought Elaine, and people would be powerless to stop it. And how many would die? she wondered. How many sick people, old people, malnourished children would die in this spell of cold weather? All over the country there were homes without heating, no fuel, no power, no way of cooking food, no winter clothes. They had never thought, in the last century, what it would be like to live in a world where everything was used up, polluted or spoiled. They had not thought what it would be like for their children and grandchildren, for future generations. How selfish they must have been, Elaine thought bitterly. But now, in a wrecked world, people knew better and so did she.

Suffering happened for a purpose, Oris had said. From grief and fears and losses, wars and catastrophes and holes in the ozone layer, lessons got learned. And yesterday on the mountains Elaine might have died had it not been for Ewan. Now, whatever hardship she might have to face, at least she was glad to be alive. But what was his experience, she wondered. She could not believe he had come there from Cardiff simply to save her life and Di's. He must have learned some lesson of his own . . . unless Bryndur had yet to teach him.

She dressed quickly. She was curious about Ewan, wanting to talk with him alone while the others were preoccupied with the morning seance. He came from a world she hardly knew — beyond the commune, beyond the valley — a different society ruled by a government, not Cilla and Oris. Things were worse out there, Alan had told her. But were they really? Elaine wanted to know.

Drifts in the orchard reached to her knees and snow blown from the branches of the apple trees showered her hair. It was all strange and beautiful but the crops would be ruined, and the curtains were still drawn in the upstairs room where Ewan slept. Elaine entered by the back door intending to wake him, but the meeting had already disbanded. Gloomy and silent the community were gathered in the kitchen and, seated in the chair by the fire, Cilla sat and wept.

'What's wrong?' asked Elaine.

'Oris,' Patti said worriedly.

'He failed to come through,' said Deirdrie.

'After all these years,' said Pru.

'Just when we need him most,' muttered Alan.

'We don't need him at all,' Elaine said callously.

'How can you say that?' Cilla wept.

'Because it's true,' said Elaine. 'He's taught us all we need to know, hasn't he? We're not children any more . . . we're adults. We don't need God, governments or Oris to tell us how to live.'

Nick frowned.

'She could be right,' he said quietly.

'Don't be ridiculous!' said Cilla.

They discussed it over the breakfast table . . . how they might survive if Oris was gone, with no reference to anyone but themselves, their own humanity and their own experience. Bryndur might have been conceived by Oris, grown and established itself under his guidance, but they *could* continue without him . . . replace the crops ruined by the weather, manure the fields, feed and clothe themselves, cut peat, grow trees. Really they no longer needed to be instructed, and they did possess certain creative and inventive faculties of their own.

'We'll manage well enough,' Alan decided.

'I don't understand!' wailed Cilla. 'Why's he left us? And where's he gone?'

They found out later when Ewan came downstairs. He would not be staying with the community, he said. He

33

had to get back to Cardiff as soon as possible. He had a housing estate to organize . . . communal kitchens, chickens in the back gardens, pigs in the garages, lawns and flowerbeds dug up for growing vegetables. People needed to be mobilized, he said. No good sitting around on their backsides watching television and trusting the government would sort things out. They had to do things for themselves and be self-sufficient.

'Like you've done here, see?' said Ewan.

'That's highly commendable,' said Alan.

'If you need someone to teach you . . .' began Nick.

'No need,' said Ewan. 'I've already got a teacher.'

'Who?' asked Elaine.

Just for a moment Ewan hesitated.

Then he told them.

A being from the fifth dimension of space and time, from the Brotherhood of the planet Hog, had made contact. He claimed to be an advanced soul and his mission on Earth was to guide people like Ewan who had not got a clue how to live. He had spent most of the night seated on the foot of his bed instructing him, and would return with him to Cardiff to make sure his instructions were carried out.

'His name's Horace,' said Ewan. 'And everything he says makes sense. I mean my life was totally meaningless until he came along. And if I hadn't caught that bus . . . what's the matter?'

In the room there was stunned silence.

Then Cilla rose to her feet.

'His name's Oris!' she screamed. 'And he's mine, not yours!'

'Really?' said Ewan. 'You want to try telling him that.'

'He's a free spirit, Cilla,' said Alan.

'He can't belong to anyone,' said Patti.

'No more than Elaine belongs to us,' said Alan.

'Or I to Alan,' said Patti.

'People aren't possessions,' said Pru.

34

'And love is not love that binds another to it,' said Deirdrie.

'Oris said that,' muttered Nick.

'So did William Blake,' said Mike.

'He can go where he will,' said Alan.

'As can we all,' confirmed Patti.

Elaine laughed in relief.

She had permission to go, permission to do as she liked, live her own life, leave the commune if she chose. Oris, simply by being himself, had set her free. Outside the snow sparkled. There were hard times ahead, yet she was free. And across the table Ewan smiled at her.

'I'm glad Oris is real,' she said.

'And you too, girlie,' Ewan replied.

2

Extinction is Forever

Vanya stared across the vast ruins of a civilization, devastated miles of tumbled concrete, twisted girders and the blackened remains of walls. It was nothing to do with the vengeance of God, Kermondley said. It was the result of a nuclear holocaust. All her life Vanya had known about the holocaust and many times she had played among the ruins of towns and cities on the edge of the lifeless land. But this time it was different or maybe she was different . . . older and more understanding. She had listened to Kermondley teaching history as once she had listened to the sea-wives telling fairy tales but now, suddenly, it all became real and she sensed the almighty meaning.

The Ancients were not simply a legendary race, just marble statues in the sea-museums, cold carved forms of men and women, artworks and artifacts and strange-sounding names. Rodin and Renoir and Richard Burton had really existed, as real and alive as she was now. Here, where the wind mourned and sighed across a loneliness of bones and dust, had been a city full of people.

'They called themselves *homo sapiens*,' Kermondley said.

'Who can tell me the meaning of *homo sapiens*?'

'Wise man?' someone said.

Kermondley nodded.

'They were joking, of course.'

The students laughed.

Everyone knew that the Ancients had engineered their own extinction. Such appalling termination was nothing to laugh at, Vanya thought. Even Kermondley showed no respect for history, no reverence for his ancestors, no grief for the various millions of life forms that had been lost. What Vanya felt was a terrible pity for the stupidity of *homo sapiens*. But all around the laughter rose like mockery, shrill as the cries of extinct birds drifting inland from the shore, carried by the wind towards the silence.

Stephen moved among the wreckage of the Third World War. The dial on his time-machine had stopped midway through the thirty-first century and time on his wrist-watch showed a quarter past noon. Two hours ago it had been 2005 and himself a student of physics at the University of London, watching the peace campaigners marching to Trafalgar Square.

'Are they right to demand the abolition of nuclear weapons?' Professor Goddard had murmured. 'Or is it, as the government claims, only the threat of nuclear war that guarantees world peace?'

Stephen shrugged, loaded the video-camera.

It took proof, not opinions, to convince governments.

'I'll bring back a film of the end of the world,' he had promised.

'I prefer to hope you will film the future of the human race,' the old professor had replied.

But that had been in 2005.

Then it was still possible to hope.

It was even possible to believe the human race had a future.

But Stephen had seen them commit the unforgivable act. He had seen the white clouds mushroom over England and the black ash falling on the land. He had witnessed the whimpering aftermath of a war they said would never happen, the hell of human dying and genetic decline. What new life was born sickened and failed . . . plant, animal and human. It seemed that nothing survived. After a thousand years there was only ruins and silence, the moan of the wind and the wash of waves against the shore. What Stephen had on film was proof of destruction, desolation without hope. But suddenly, far away and strangely incongruous . . . he heard laughter.

'Don't laugh at them!' Vanya cried.

It was an odd thing to say, an odd reaction . . . as if she believed the Ancients listened, a city full of ghostly souls made vulnerable by genocide and shame. There were tears in her eyes as she turned away. And then Kermondley understood . . . Vanya had realized that history had really happened and all his years of teaching were suddenly worthwhile.

He watched her swim towards the shore, the line of wharfs and rusting wrecks of ships and fallen warehouses. He saw her reach the flight of crumbled steps, her webbed hands heaving herself up in one lithe arching motion of water and light, reflections of sky on wet scales.

'Where's she going?' someone asked him.

'Do we follow?' asked another.

Kermondley shook his head.

He remembered himself at Vanya's age. He remembered the moment when history had come alive for him too. In another city, just like this one, he had felt the anguish of the Ancients dying, heard the scream of unborn generations echoing through time. He too had been felled by feelings of horror and grief. But now Kermondley could laugh at the arrogance of those who had called themselves wise . . . for his kind had been formed among the ashes of their world and he was glad they had not survived.

Stephen walked towards the sound of distant voices, his footsteps silent in the dust. He came to water and acres of drowned streets, a great river estuary where Thames-side London had been. In a stench of seaweed and barnicles he saw her haul herself on to the land. He realized then that she was human . . . or had been.

He closed his eyes, leaned against the vitrified remains of a doorpost, waited for the horror and repulsion to subside and his thoughts to become rational. He should have expected it. He should have known if anything survived the holocaust it was bound to be a mutation. He remembered the banners the peace campaigners had carried . . . EXTINCTION IS FOREVER, they said.

And maybe it was not enough to build a time-machine, not enough to present the governments of the world with evidence of genocide. Maybe it would not persuade them to disarm. And simply by establishing their nuclear arsenals they had already accepted the possibility that untold millions of people would die. The public too had already accepted it. Mass destruction was a box-office hit. Earthquakes, infernos, nuclear war itself was being shown in every local cinema. People actually paid to watch it!

Sometimes Stephen believed that the human race was willing its own annihilation, that it was a suicide instinct triggered naturally whenever the species put too great a strain upon the environment. Rabbits failed to breed . . . lemmings flung themselves from a cliff and drowned in the sea . . . and human beings went to war. It was a biological fail-safe, a way of preserving the species by reducing the number of individuals. But this time they would go too far.

Extinction was forever.

But maybe if they knew what they would become . . .

Stephen raised the video-camera.

This was the hope Professor Goddard had asked for. This was the future of the human race, a true daughter of the holocaust . . . a scaly mutant, mackerel-coloured, sea-dwelling. And out in the estuary a whole shoal of them!

Vanya let the dry dust trickle through her fingers. The past belonged to her and all that once lived was as real and precious as she was now. She saw a sungleam break through the clouds, gold light touching the crumbled heart of the city, making it sacred. The stillness was so intense she was almost afraid. Out in the estuary the swimmers turned towards the distant beach. Vanya was tempted to rejoin them but something moved within the darkness of a broken doorway. Something emerged from the shadows and became a man.

Homo sapiens was not extinct!

The camera whirred and clicked.

And Vanya's voice was a scream across the open water.

'Kermondley! Come back!'

Stephen gaped at her.

Her voice was beautiful, clear as a bell or a bird call, a sonar echo or a siren's song . . . each word pure and distinct in perfect English. She was not some kind of human sub-species. She was a being in her own right who perceived and communicated and was aware. Her bright aquamarine eyes regarded him nervously, the curiosity tinged with fear.

'I won't hurt you,' Stephen assured her.

One webbed finger pointed to the camera.

'You carry a weapon!' she said.

'It's a video-machine,' he corrected.

'You used to kill,' she said. 'All the Ancients did. They killed everything that lived upon the land, including themselves.'

'Hell!' said Stephen. 'Is that all that has survived of us . . . our blasted murderous reputation?'

Kermondley would never know what caused him to look back. Perhaps unconsciously he heard her cry or sensed her fear. For a while he could see nothing but the dazzle of light on water and waves swilling around the broken dome of St Paul's cathedral. But then on the skyline of land he saw that Vanya was not alone. Someone was with her, framed in a sunlit doorway . . . the dark silhouette of a man.

Kermondley blinked.

He was reminded of the small bronze statuette he had dredged from the silt of sunken towns around Southampton water. But this was no museum piece. This man was alive . . . a figure that moved as Vanya moved, approached as she retreated, paused and raised his hands in the age-old gesture of peace and surrender.

Above the drowned spans of antique bridges Kermondley trod water and could not believe his eyes. The Ancients had become extinct a thousand years ago . . . like dodos and mastodons they were gone from the world. World-over the land had decayed to deserts of dust, supported no life larger than lizards and sand-flies and forests of sparse vegetation that clung to the rivers' reaches. Not even birds had survived. Yet Kermondley saw a man.

He called the students back.

'Tell me I'm dreaming,' Kermondley said.

They looked at him, puzzled.

'Over on the shore where Vanya is . . . what do you see?' Kermondley asked them. 'What do you make of that shape in the doorway that looks to me like a man?'

'Everything died of radiation,' Vanya said. 'But the oceans diffused it and the seas contained our only source of food. So we had to adapt and become aquatic. We had to hunt the shoals of fish hundreds of miles from the nearest shore, and cultivate seaweed . . .'

Stephen stared at her.

It was not mutation she talked of.

It was evolution.

Natural selection, which should have taken millions of years, had created a different species within a few generations. Men had to swim for survival . . . their skin

41

turning to scales, feet to flippers. Now, looking at Vanya, not much remained of her human ancestry . . . just her voice, her aquamarine eyes and the pale breasts that made her female.

'Do you breed underwater?' he asked her.

Vanya felt embarrassed.

The way Stephen looked at her, the way he questioned her . . . it was as if he regarded her as some kind of biological specimen, as if sea-people were no different from dolphins or seals. Maybe he imagined her among a colony, hauled up like sea-cows on a barren beach to wait for the breeding season. He did not seem to realize . . .

'There are cities under the sea,' she said primly.

'Half of London by the look of it,' Stephen said.

'Not ruins!' said Vanya. 'Living cities! Pressurised domes full of warmth and light! Sea-gardens bloom beyond our windows in colours like the land has never known. We have music and drama, museums and galleries and schools of learning. Under the sea we eat and sleep and, yes, we breed.'

An underwater civilization!

Incredulity showed on Stephen's face, turned to nervousness as he saw Kermondley recrossing the estuary, his dark shape speeding through the water followed by a dozen more. Suddenly Stephen realized that *he* was the alien, the intruder, out of place and out of time. And if the sea-people could build cities under the ocean they were even more accomplished than the human race, more advanced, more intelligent . . . maybe more dangerous.

Muscles rippled, flashed and shone with blue-green sheen as Kermondley gained the lower steps and started to climb. Stephen backed away. Stones from a wall slipped and fell as he knocked against it and the video-camera hung heavy and useless around his neck. He wished he had brought a gun or a harpoon . . . something to defend himself with . . . anything. His fingers gripped a jagged lump of concrete as the rest of the sea-people crowded on to the land.

'Stay right where you are!' Stephen howled.

Vanya laughed.

'We're all quite harmless,' she said. 'It's only the history class and Kermondley who teaches us. He always said history was alive but I bet he never expected to meet a real live *homo sapien* who should have been extinct!'

Kermondley stopped, not because he was afraid of being struck by a lump of concrete but because he sensed the Ancient was afraid. He probably recognized the sea-people as aquatic descendants of his own race and expected them to display the same mistrust, the same tendency to attack first and ask questions afterwards. He motioned the students to stay behind him, waited as Vanya laughed her reassurances, then bowed his head in greeting. Not by the flicker of an eyelid did Kermondley betray his own, more terrible fear.

'Be welcome, *homo sapien*,' Kermondley said.

'His name's Stephen,' said Vanya.

'And we were hardly wise,' Stephen admitted.

Kermondley smiled.

'It's a little late to realize that, my friend.'

'Not where I come from,' Stephen said.

'Space?' Kermondley asked hopefully.

'Time,' said Stephen. '2005.'

Kermondley nodded.

His fear was established now.

'I thought perhaps you had returned from the stars,' Kermondley said. 'A space traveller cryogenically frozen for ten centuries. I didn't know the Ancients actually invented a machine that could travel time.'

'Officially we haven't,' Stephen told him.

'But unofficially you have?' Kermondley prompted.

It was Stephen's turn to smile.

43

Apart from himself no one knew they had invented a time-machine, either officially or unofficially. Even Professor Goddard waiting in the laboratory could not know until Stephen returned. Government departments, heads of the armed services and scientists all over the world waited with bated breaths. Should time travel become a proven reality, its effects on the past and future of the human race seemed virtually unlimited.

'This is our first experiment,' Stephen said. 'We needed to know what would happen in the future in order to prevent it. Many of us predicted it, of course, but now I have proof.' He patted the video-camera. 'Proof of the war and what happens afterwards . . . you and Vanya and all of this.'

Kermondley understood.

Stephen's eyes said what his words did not, stared bitterly and fixedly out across the estuary to the fallen dome of the cathedral. He could not accept human extinction. He would return to his own time, present his evidence of the future, and the nuclear holocaust would never happen. The London Stephen loved would rise again from the sea and all Kermondley's kind would never exist.

The thought touched Vanya too, triggered the same fear. She had always accepted the legacy of barren land and living ocean and never wished it could be different . . . but Stephen did. Stephen hated everything he saw because all he saw was the terrible ruin of his own world, his own civilization. He did not see Vanya's world . . . the green perpetual beauty and peace of the undersea cities. He did not understand how good it was to be alive in the present time. He just wanted it gone . . . everything restored to what it was. Stephen was trying to change the future and it did not occur to him that his future was Vanya's past.

'History is a living process,' Kermondley had said.

Vanya could feel it.

History contained inside herself.

For her the universe had formed and spread. For her the Earth revolved around the sun and life evolved. She was the reason why countless millions of species had become extinct. She was the reason why the Ancients had dropped their bombs and died over decades of terror and pain. The whole of history had happened that she might exist.

'And no one can change it,' Vanya thought. 'No one can change history!'

But maybe Stephen could.

Across the dusty space of land she met Kermondley's gaze, teacher and pupil in a moment of recognition. The thought was the same in both of them. But she was the only one on the landward side, the only one who could act. Vanya hesitated, appalled by the awfulness of what she must do. But Kermondley's eyes urged her, willed her to go. She turned away, searched for Stephen's footprints in the dust and followed them into the city.

Stephen squatted on his heels on the cliff edge of the street, watching the water swill against the old foundations, a slow relentless erosion. The ebb tide left its line of green weed on the dome of St Paul's and sea voices whispered around him, alien, inhuman, Kermondley's students crowding the steps, restless and waiting. Stephen had been in their time for less than half an hour and already he had seen all he wanted to see and was ready to go. The loneliness depressed him, the immense absence of everything he knew. The silence grated on his nerves. He had no reason to stay in this godforsaken future any longer but Kermondley delayed him.

'This being a history lesson,' Kermondley said, 'we would like to take this unique opportunity . . . would you mind?'

'Sure,' said Stephen. 'What can I tell you?'

'What was it really like in 2005?' one of the students asked.

They had no idea.

They could not even imagine trees in St James's Park or Christmas lights glittering along Oxford Street. They had never tasted potato chips or strawberries and cream. They had never smelled roses, touched cat's fur, heard a blackbird sing, ridden the fun-fair rides or the rush-hour train. All the things Stephen took for granted were meaningless to them.

Surrounded by ocean and empty lands, Kermondley's students could grasp very little of everyday human existence. It was like trying to describe colours to people born blind, or spinning them fairy tales. They had thought all Ancients were violent, that everyone went around attacking everyone else, that tanks and guns and atom bombs were personal possessions. It was not easy to convince them that most Ancients had not wanted war.

'If no one wanted it how come it happened?' they asked.

'Maybe it won't,' he said.

'It already has,' said Kermondley.

'Not in my time,' said Stephen. 'In 2005 we can still prevent it and my evidence will make the vital difference. Now I must go. It's been nice meeting you.'

He turned towards the ruins of the city.

Vanya stood in the broken doorway.

Sea-green tears shimmered in her eyes.

'I'll wait for you, Stephen,' Vanya said.

And he thought she was crazy.

No one waited for a thousand years!

The future was dependent on the past.

If anyone should change the past . . .

'We had to make sure,' Kermondley said.

'There was nothing he could have done,' said Vanya. 'We know that because we're here! If he had succeeded we wouldn't exist!'

'We had to make sure,' Kermondley repeated.

'One nuclear war guaranteed,' Vanya said bitterly.

'The Ancients still have a choice,' Kermondley reminded her.

'Stephen doesn't,' she said dully.

Kermondley sighed.

'At least he's alive.'

But Vanya knew that being alive would be no consolation to Stephen. Heavy on her conscience was the sick knowledge of what she had done to him. She followed Kermondley down the steps. Her skin felt itchy and dry. She needed the silk sweet water to wash the dust from her scales. She needed to swim away, far out to sea, and forget.

Her fellow students waited and called.

'Hurry up, Vanya!'

'It's way past lunchtime!'

'And Kermondley said we can go!'

'We'll race you to the restaurant!'

'Are you coming?'

'You go,' Kermondley said quietly. 'I'll wait for Stephen.'

Vanya shook her head.

She too would wait.

And his cry rose from the heart of the ruined city making a pain in her heart like she had never known before. It was a cry of anguish and despair that went on and on, a terrible human sound. Vanya sobbed inconsolably knowing what he had found. She had smashed the workings of his time-machine. He was trapped here now for the rest of his life . . . *homo sapiens* on the verge of extinction, the only one of his kind.

Professor Goddard switched off the laboratory light and closed the door. He had waited all afternoon and evening but Stephen had not come back. The experiment had failed. His theory of time travel remained unproven and a young man was missing, presumed dead.

Professor Goddard sighed and shook his head. It was

not only guilt that troubled him. He also knew the consequences of academic failure. He would not get a second chance to build a time-machine. His research grant would not be renewed and he would have to accept retirement from the university, an old discredited scientist exiled to a bungalow in Bognor Regis . . . growing zinnias perhaps.

He sighed again, buttoned his jacket and went out into the night. He was just one more old man whose life had not amounted to very much. He did not read the writing on the banner that someone had tied to the front railings.

EXTINCTION IS FOREVER, it said.

3

A Love Song for Arni

Rhiannon was an Earth child, of Welsh extraction. The land of her father, her grandfather, mists and mountains, valleys and song, was etched in her soul although she had never been there. It was simply a tale told of genetic origins, photographs in an album, a kind of love. Long ago her parents and grandparents had left it, emigrants heading outwards into the galaxy to richer worlds, not wanting to return. It was legend now, light-years away, but in a moment of remembering they called their child Rhiannon.

She had been born on a star cruiser . . . her mother the Captain, her father the First Engineer. Virtually she was weaned on to navigational computers and hyper-space technology, and learned to toddle in the shining corridors and glittering passenger lounges. The ship carried tourists from star system to star system on two-year trips, ferried them to various planets for brief excursions . . . to the waterfalls on Carridon and Earoth's palaces, the Banjulian Bazaars and the Art Galleries on Mew. Worlds were like flowers to Rhiannon, passing wonders, visited and gone. Her home the distances between stars.

She was not deprived in any way, except of parental company. In between shifts they cared for her well enough, but most of her time was spent in the crêche and then the kindergarten, and the on board school-rooms when she grew. She formed a few transitory friendships with children of her own age, off-spring of passengers who came and went, but she was always beyond them. Mostly she preferred the company of the crew . . . Mucky, who cleaned the cabins, and the Chief Steward in his starched white coat, whiskered Sam in charge of provisions and Denny who organized the entertainments. It was Denny who took her to the Interstellar Song Contest on Penda.

Rhiannon was seven years old at the time, a small girl emerging from the landing craft with a group of tourists, clutching the hand of a uniformed officer and sitting beside him on the rows of tiered seats that encircled the arena. Blue-velvet dusk over a vast amphitheatre, the sky deepening to purple as Penda's star set, coloured strobe lights dancing like rainbows in the air. It was thrilling, magical . . . a hum of voices all around, gleams of alien eyes and warm summer darkness . . . more magical still when the music began.

The crowd grew hushed.

And a single spotlight followed the first competitor.

'Arni of Goth!' the announcer said dramatically.

He was small and far away, indiscernable except for the whiteness of his shirt. But the vision screens showed him in close-up — a boy perched on a high stool with a steel guitar. He was older than Rhiannon — eleven, maybe twelve years of age. Dark his countenance, and his teeth flashed white as he smiled. He seemed to be smiling directly at her. And he sang for her . . . a traditional love song from the desert people of Kahl, he said. Soft and slow the guitar strummed through her nerves and his voice made a pain inside her, although she did not understand the words or the meaning. Spellbound she listened, wanting him to sing forever. But it ended too soon and he made his exit to a roar of applause.

Rhiannon clapped until her hands hurt.

'Will he sing again?' she asked Denny.

'Only if he wins,' Denny informed her.

'When will that be?'

'At the end of the Junior Section.'

'Why can't he sing again now?'

'Because he hasn't won yet.'

'I want to sing like him,' said Rhiannon.

'Hush,' said Denny. 'We're here to listen, not talk.'

Rhiannon fidgeted, not really interested any more. The girl was not the same as Arni of Goth, nor anyone else who followed. Their songs, their voices, made no impression. And no impression on the judges either for in the end Arni won easily, the youngest ever to compete in the Song Contest on Penda.

She took it away with her, a repeat performance, his smile in her mind and the echoes of his song. A bi-annual event, said Denny. It would be two long years before the next Song Contest and Rhiannon heard Arni sing again, but she would not forget him. He was a part of her now, her joy at his triumph, the thrill of the audience and the gold glittering medallion he had won. She was only a child but he set a dream in her head. And back on the star cruiser, in the Captain's suite of cabins, she did not hesitate to announce it.

'I want to sing,' she said.

Her mother smiled indulgently.

'Go on then.'

'No!' said Rhiannon. 'I mean I want to sing properly. I want to sing in the Song Contest on Penda and I want a guitar.'

Rhiannon pestered.

She could not sing properly without a guitar.

And, knowing her own desire, she was insistant.

A childish whim, said her mother, that should not be given in to. Or it could be a latent ability, her father argued. His side of the family had always been musical. On the next planet they visited, in the teeming markets among street vendors' cries, he bought her a Banjulian guitar.

It was not the same as Arni's. Its tone was softer, its black wood brightly painted. But Rhiannon loved it anyway, although she had no idea how to play. She only thought she could, an instantaneous maestro discordantly strumming. To her untrained ear it was a perfect sound, in harmony with her voice which was shrill and completely tuneless. Armed with a repertoire of traditional nursery rhymes, she sought an audience.

Leaving a planet was always a busy time. Her mother was on the bridge, distracted and unwilling to listen. And in the engineering department her father was occupied with the main drive units. Sam was shifting boxes of fresh fruit to the kitchens. Mucky was still cleaning cabins and Denny was rehearsing a troupe of veiled dancers. 'Not now, Rhiannon,' everyone said.

Rhiannon went busking then, entertained the passengers in the main lounge. They applauded politely at first. Then, one by one, they drifted away. And the same thing happened in the bar, and the games room, and the coffee shop.

'Clear off, Rhiannon!' said the Chief Steward.

She took to the corridors after that.

A wandering minstrel . . . until Denny found her. Passengers were complaining about the noise, he said.

'It's not noise! It's singing!' Rhiannon said indignantly.

'You could have fooled me!' Denny replied.

Rhiannon was crushed.

She did not understand. People liked Arni's music, travelled light-years to hear him sing. So why was she banned from all public areas of the ship? Why did Sam wince? And Mucky frown? And the Chief Steward send her to the hangar deck out of earshot? It was dark down there. Dim lights shone eerily on a dozen small landing craft. But the acoustics were good, her voice all loud and echoey. Only the guitar was not quite right. Its strings twanged limply and she fiddled with the keys.

'Give it to me, little girl,' said a man.

Rhiannon clutched it.

'No!' she said defiantly.

'I show you how to tune it,' he offered.

52

His name was Ebo. He was a trainee mechanic who had been born on Banjuli and, watching him turn the tuning keys, listening to him strum and sing, Rhiannon suddenly realized her own ignorance. It was a quick hot moment of humiliation. She had wailed her awfulness around the whole ship for everyone to hear when really she could neither play nor sing. Tears filled her eyes. She would never do it again, she thought. But Ebo smiled encouragingly. She had a good little voice if she learned how to pitch and give it expression, he said, and the guitar was a beautiful instrument if she learned how to play.

'You want I should teach you, little girl?'

Rhiannon stared at him.

All her dreams came rushing back . . . a vision of Arni and the strobe lights dancing, herself standing beside him with the gold medallion around her neck, the applause of the audience and the flashing whiteness of his smile. He would be glad when she won, just as she had been glad for him. And Ebo offered to teach her.

'Yes, please,' she said.

'Tomorrow,' said Ebo.

'And I won't tell my mother,' said Rhiannon.

It was the start of a relationship, a secret between Ebo and herself. Each day, after the end of her conventional schooling, Rhiannon fetched her guitar from the cabin and went to the hangar deck. She was impatient at first, wanting to learn everything at once. But music was slow, said Ebo, as slow as her own growth and as precise as the stars in their orbits, a perfect balance of sound. She must practise and practise and learn to listen until her voice matched the tone of each plucked string, exact and perfect.

It was not easy. Rhiannon could not sing in tune, or strum a single chord with competence. The sound buzzed and blurred and the thin strings cut into her fingers until every touch was a pain. She wanted to cry with her own uselessness and smash the guitar against the wall, but something inside her refused to give in. And gradually she improved. Her fingers hardened, began to move instinctively of their own accord over the frets and strings. And her mind listened, approved or disapproved, noting each small imperfection.

Six months went by.

A year . . . almost two.

'You're getting good, little girl,' said Ebo.

'And why are your school results so poor?' asked her mother.

Computers were boring, Rhiannon thought, and she had already learned all she wanted to learn about hyperspace technology. But it was too late then to announce herself. The next Song Contest on Penda was only weeks away and she had missed the preliminary rounds. Once again she accompanied Denny, sat beside him on the tiered seats among a group of tourists. It was another warm summer night, the same blue velvet sky, the same stars and the strobe lights dancing, just as she remembered. But this time Rhiannon was older, nine years old, and was aware of a different magic.

This time it was not the atmosphere that thrilled and captivated, but the skill of each performer, their musical ability, their voice quality, their choice of song . . . always traditional from the cultures of a dozen different planets. She watched them intently, listened intently, appreciated and applauded every youth, every girl. And then Arni sang — a tall gangly boy of fourteen — his performance less raw, more dramatic than before, and his song even more beautiful. It was wild and rhythmical, from a gypsy tribe of the Dellos star system five hundred light-years away where Rhiannon had never been. She knew he must win; and he did, for the second time.

'Arni of Goth!' cried the announcer.

Again Rhiannon was glad for him, an adoring child among an adoring audience, with a joy inside her, loving his laughter on the vision screens, the triumph flashing from his eyes, the dark curl of his hair. She bought a poster of him from a souvenir stall to pin on her cabin wall, and a cassette of his songs which she could play over and over until she saw him again. Two years seemed a very long time. But by then, she decided, she would be good enough to compete. And she might even win. She filled in an entry form before she left but she did not tell her mother.

Ebo frowned.

'I think you should tell her quick, little girl.'

'I want to surprise her,' Rhiannon said.

'And how you going to do it?' Ebo asked her. 'How you going to do it on your own? You've gone and entered the big time and that's not singing for fun like we're doing here. You need help, little girl.'

'What I need is a song,' Rhiannon said obstinately.

With a child's confidence Rhiannon did as she wanted, and so did Ebo. He taught her a selection of Banjulian street ballads and she practised them diligently alone in her cabin with the poster of Arni smiling at her from the wall above her bed. Almost it became a way of life. Friendships ceased to matter and conventional schooling did not count for very much. All she needed was Arni and the songs she sang for him and comments from Ebo to help improve her playing. Mucky complained that she never kept him company any more. And Sam asked curiously where she went and what she did. And Denny asked what Ebo had that he did not.

'Nothing,' said Rhiannon.

'You can't keep secrets on a star ship,' Denny told her.

'Give us a tune,' said the Chief Steward.

Rhiannon refused.

She was not yet ready for an official audience.

Then, several weeks later, a message was received by the ship's radio-communications officer. Rhiannon was to attend a preliminary song contest on Grath-Beta.

Automatically it was relayed to the Captain. And that was the first her mother had heard of Rhiannon's musical bent since the first bald announcement of a seven-year-old girl that she wanted to sing. That evening, in the suite of cabins that formed their family living quarters, she confronted her daughter, angrily slammed the computer print-out on the table.

'What's this?' the Captain demanded.

'Notification,' mumbled Rhiannon.

'And how are you going to get to Grath-Beta?'

'Probably she hopes you'll take her,' said her father.

'I see,' said the Captain. 'You know all about it, do you?'

'Not exactly,' said her father.

And the argument began.

Grath-Beta was not on the visiting list, her mother declared. It was two dozen light-years off course and they had a schedule to keep. Rhiannon could not sing to that kind of standard anyway, let alone play a musical instrument. She had hardly touched the Banjulian guitar her father had bought her. But down in the engineering department there had been rumours. A trainee mechanic by the name of Ebo had taught Rhiannon to play. She was a talented child, apparently, and needed their support.

'Not every girl has ambitions to be a starship captain,' said Rhiannon's father.

'She's a natural technician,' said her mother.

'Music *is* technical,' said her father.

'And where will it get her?'

'If it's what she wants . . .'

'She's hardly old enough to know!'

'At least we can listen!'

'All right!' said the Captain. 'All right, I'll listen. Go and fetch your guitar, Rhiannon. And you had better be good!'

Rhiannon fetched it from the tiny cabin that was her bedroom. She felt sick with nervousness, knowing what it meant to perform before her mother, the rest of her life dependent on a single song. The Banjulian street ballad was quite familiar, a song she had sung and played many times before. But her throat felt dry and her hands trembled, her voice wavered and she could not remember a sequence of chords. Stars streaked past the porthole window as she stumbled into silence.

'I'm sorry,' Rhiannon muttered.

'Judges don't accept apologies,' her mother said curtly.

'Try again,' urged her father.

Rhiannon bent her head.

And this time she forgot about *them*. There was only herself and the song that flowed through her, the words and the music, her fingers on the strings. Her voice grew sure and strong, although she hardly heard it. Her whole being was focussed on the sweet finger-picking style, the exactness of rhythm and timing, as if nothing else existed. And when it was over and the significance came rushing back to her, she knew she could not have played any better.

'That was very good,' her father said warmly.

'Yes,' agreed her mother.

And it was all she needed to say.

It was an odd sort of life Rhiannon led then, plying between planets, mixing technology with music, songs with stars. The passengers seemed not to mind the unscheduled stops. She was the Captain's daughter and she sang for them each evening aboard the star cruiser so they knew her well, followed her progress keenly. In various concert halls around the galaxy, through all the qualifying rounds, they were there to applaud her . . . her own personal audience.

They were there for the Song Contest on Penda, too. Rhiannon could actually feel them among the dark sea of faces, a little group of people willing her to win. She was the youngest competitor yet, the announcer said. But in the vast open-air arena she was overwhelmed. Her voice was too thin and small, her song too well-known, the guitar too dominant. She could not compete with others of her class, and none of them could compete with Arni of Goth.

Rhiannon watched him from the wings. He stood on the central dais, his arms raised in triumph, the gold medallion hung around his neck for the third successive time. He was dark and proud and had not even noticed her. Placed last, she supposed she was not worth noticing. But he was always like that, an older girl told her, arrogant and sure of his own success. A big-head, said a boy, someone who thought himself better than everyone else. Defeat made them bitter and for a while Rhiannon lost heart. Thinking she could never be as good as Arni, she decided she might as well give up.

But the passengers consoled her.

'Never mind,' they said.

'You did very well.'

'We're very proud of you.'

'You can't expect to be better than Arni of Goth.'

'But you might win a place next time.'

'So you mustn't give up.'

'Not ever, little girl,' said Ebo.

Ebo had taught her all he knew and was no more use. Rhiannon turned to her parents. She persuaded them to pay for professional training, three terms in a musical academy to improve her voice. And in the next Song. Contest on Penda Rhiannon was placed second. Her score was almost as good as Arni's for artistic ability and technical accomplishment, but again her song was too familiar, a folk song from Carridon, well-loved but unoriginal, losing her marks. She ought to try a Federation television jingle, Arni said sarcastically.

It was the first time he had spoken to her and his criticism brought tears to her eyes. He was probably afraid she might win the next contest and was trying to demoralize her, said the girl beside her. Or maybe he cared, thought Rhiannon. Maybe, musically, he wanted to lift her to the heights he had reached. He wanted to be as moved by her song as she was by his, love lyrics piercing her like starlight or pain, cold as snow from the ice planet of Cos.

'How did he know where to find it?' Rhiannon asked.

'He goes hunting,' said the girl.

'All over the galaxy searching for songs,' said a boy.

'Alone?' asked Rhiannon.

'With his father,' said the girl.

'Not now,' said the boy. 'He's got his own ship.'

Rhiannon sighed.

It would be another three years before she could apply for a licence and pilot her own solo craft. And although her mother ferried her to the various song contests, no way would she take her around the galaxy searching for songs. She would have to make do with Ebo's street ballads, or songs heard by chance on the planets she visited. But almost the song seemed not to matter any more. Arni qualified for the Adult Section now and Rhiannon's victory was a foregone conclusion. Next time on Penda she won easily, a gold medallion and a cheque for ten thousand galactic dollars. But somehow it seemed a hollow victory. Far greater was Arni's on the following night, at nineteen claiming for himself the coveted minstrel's crown.

'Arni of Goth!' the announcer cried.

And Rhiannon sighed again.

She dreamed of the moment he would truly notice her, when her song warmed his heart and the white flashing smile that charmed whole audiences would be turned on her. She imagined his dark eyes gazing into hers and the first touch of his hand. He would accept her as an equal and maybe they would sing together, become a duo. And she could not believe what was said of him, that he was cruel and callous, a singer without a soul who only cared about winning. It was jealousy or chagrin, she thought, that prompted such snide remarks. No one could sing as Arni sang and not have a soul. And she needed a love song . . . a love song for Arni to tell him how she felt.

'A love song?' said Denny.

'Traditional,' said Rhiannon.

'I know one or two.'

'Teach me,' said Rhiannon.

And she was not a child any more when she returned to Penda two years later. She was seventeen, driving her own small ship, and competing as a junior for the last time. Again she won, but again her victory seemed meaningless, the gold medallion no more than an endorsement for all her years of hard work. It was earned, along with the applause.

'Goodbye, Rhiannon,' the announcer said.

And she stepped from the dais to face the rest of her life.

And Arni.

He was waiting in the wings, a young man in a white shirt, his dark eyes fixed on her face. Rhiannon held her breath. This was the moment she had been waiting for, dreamed of, longed for. He had come to congratulate her, she thought. But he did not smile. His lips twisted in a sneer of disdain.

'What a pathetic song,' he said.

Rhiannon stared at him.

Disappointment seered through her.

Then anger.

'*I* like it,' she retorted.

' "The Londonderry Air"!' scoffed Arni. 'And what will it be next time? "Lavender's Blue"? You'll be competing against me, remember? And if you want my advice you'll spare yourself the humiliation and not bother to enter.'

He turned and walked away.

And Rhiannon's anger blazed into fury as she followed him.

Her voice was a scream among the crowds milling outside the stadium.

'You're never going to win again, Arni of Goth!'

He did, of course. On the following night he won the minstrel's crown for the second time, Arni whom Rhiannon had loved and idolized for so many years bowing to the crowds, kissing his hands and gathering up the flowers. Spotlights dimmed as he made his exit, and the applause went on, thousands of voices calling him back. For the last time, Rhiannon thought bitterly, as she returned to her ship. And she had never thought about winning before, never wanted it, not for herself. But she did now. She would do anything, anything to defeat Arni of Goth.

In the landing park she waited for Arni to depart. Where he went, she would go, taking the same flight paths to the same planets. And next time on Penda her song would match his, words and music come from the same source. 'I shan't be coming back on board,' she told the orbiting star cruiser. And she took off, five seconds behind Arni, with a blast of fire.

Over the radio her mother was scathing.

Rhiannon was far too young and inexperienced to go haring across the galaxy alone. Planet-hopping was a dangerous occupation. If she had any sense she would return to the star cruiser immediately. And what about her education?

'What about it?' Rhiannon asked.

'You need to think about your career!'

'*This* is my career!'

'What you're doing has got damn all to do with music or art!'

'You know nothing about it and nor have you ever really cared!' Rhiannon retorted.

'Have you thought what might happen to you, a young girl all on her own?'

'I'm not going alone! I'm going with Arni!'

'Who's Arni?'

'If you took an interest you'd know.'

'A man, I suppose.'

'A singer,' said Rhiannon. 'Like me, Mother.'

'And you'll throw up everything? For an infatuation?'

'It's my life!' said Rhiannon. 'And anyway it's not like that.'

'Well,' snapped her mother. 'If you end up in trouble don't come crying to me!'

Rhiannon switched off.

She did not need her mother any more. She was old enough to do as she pleased and go where she liked. She would be safe enough planet-hopping with Arni nearby, she thought. He might be a louse but he would not stand by and watch anything bad happen to her. Confident and sure of herself, Rhiannon checked her instruments and set a course.

Arni though, knew nothing of her intentions. He simply heard rumours that she, like him, was staying on Korberon with the nomad tribes, recording their songs. And coincidentally he also saw her several times in the cities on Rhune, sipping fruit juices in the brawling bars and listening to the music. Not until he noticed the small bleep of her ship trailing him among the stars did Arni realize.

Angrily he opened the communications channel.

'Are you following me?'

'Why would I want to do that?' Rhiannon inquired.

His reply was lost in a crackle of static.

Then it came clear.

'Push off!' he told her.

'I don't take orders from you!' Rhiannon said. 'And it's a free universe so I can go where I please!'

'We'll see about that!' Arni said savagely.

His ship was a speck among stars.

Then it was not.

Black emptiness showed on her scanners. He had made the jump into hyper-space and was trying to lose her. Quickly Rhiannon made her own jump, cutting through curving corridors of light, following the faint heat traces of radiation. But her passage was slower in the second-hand ship and when she emerged into the stillness of another solar system there was no sign of Arni.

Unknown worlds revolved around an unknown sun and Rhiannon had no idea where she was. She fed her co-ordinates into the computer and consulted the star charts. Nothing was named in that part of the galaxy apart from the planet Taska. Rhiannon frowned. The name was vaguely familiar, although she could not remember how or why or where she had heard it before. And it was listed as uninhabitable . . . a breathable atmosphere but all marsh and mountains and useless for colonization. But there were minerals there. And where there were minerals there would be mines and men singing songs as they worked. Arni must have gone there, Rhiannon concluded, and set her ship in orbit for a surface scan.

Low cloud obscured her view, drizzling rain every-where and no break in it for hours. By infra-red she located half a dozen encampments, and Arni could have been at any one of them. She had no way of telling. Then, finally, towards evening when the mists began to clear, she spotted his ship. Sleek silver in the sunset light, it was parked at the foot of a mountain range and swiftly, before the daylight faded, she prepared for her own landing.

Wherever Arni was, he must have seen her, bright jets of flame sinking slowly downwards, her ship touching land only a few hundred metres away from his. Perfect, thought Rhiannon. But it was not perfect enough. Suddenly, with a sound of tearing metal, it tilted at an angle, sank and settled in a bog. Her stomach lurched, and warily she opened the hatch. Mud lapped at the sill with a stench of rotting weed, and a damage check showed a broken tail fin, her ship unable to take off.

'Arni!' shrieked Rhiannon.

No one answered.

And no one answered over the radio either. Arni, it seemed, was not on board. Only the marsh birds called plaintively across the distances and the wind played like music in the reeds. Or was it human music she could hear and the glow of a night fire high up the mountain? Rhiannon did not have time to be sure. Crowds of midges came swarming towards her and she had to retreat and close the door. There was no choice then but to stay in the cabin, watch through the scanners as darkness fell, and wait for Arni's return.

Cloud and rain obscured the moon and stars and Rhiannon slept fitfully, dozed and woke and dozed again, until a sound disturbed her. It was dawn outside, drizzling grey light, and she heard a ship taking off. Panic drove her into action. She opened the hatch and desperately screamed his name, but she was already too late. His ship lifted slowly through the mist in a gleam of silver and a blast of fire, its noise drowning her cry. 'Take me with you, Arni! Please don't go!' No hope he could hear her. Her words were stupid, ineffectual, and she could only watch, helplessly, the tail flames diminishing, vanishing, until nothing remained but rain and silence and her own tears.

How could he do it? she thought. How could he go and leave her stranded on this godforsaken planet? He must have known her ship was damaged. He must have known she could not take off. And all these years she had admired him, been glad for him, applauded him, learned to sing and play, a girl with a dream striving to match him, wanting him to notice her, wanting him to care. Because of him she had lived in a stinking tent on Korberon. She had gone alone into the various drinking houses on Rhune where anything might have happened. And she had followed him here, to Taska, not really because she wanted to win, but because she cared.

64

But he cared nothing for her, not even as one human being for another.

He was an unfeeling swine, thought Rhiannon.

He was a worm, a rat, a toad.

Or maybe he was not.

'This way, young lady.'

She turned her head.

She saw a group of men standing on the edge of dry land, shapes in the mist with planks and ropes, come there to rescue her. The young man had told them where to find her, they said. Gratefully Rhiannon fetched her guitar, tied the rope around her waist and stepped out. The planks sank and tilted under her weight and mud oozed over the tops of her shoes as the men hauled her to safety. She assumed they were miners, although they were hardly dressed like miners. Their clothes were too colourful. They wore bright silk shirts and scarves, earrings and nose studs and polished leather boots. Gypsies, thought Rhiannon. But then she remembered why Taska had seemed familiar. Once, aboard her mother's ship, she had heard a traveller telling tales of a horde of outlaws living there.

'This way, young lady.'

'Who *are* you?' Rhiannon asked suspiciously.

The men laughed and exchanged glances.

'We're scrap metal merchants,' said one.

'Dealers in broken-down space craft,' said another.

'Entrepreneurs,' said a third.

'We do what it pays us to do.'

'And it pays us to look after you.'

'An accident, perhaps?'

'Sunk in the marshes?'

'Gone without trace?'

'Fifty thousand dollars, the young man paid us.'

'Plus your ship.'

Rhiannon stared at them in horror.

'You mean Arni wants me dead?'

'Missing,' said a man. 'Just missing, he said.'

'Dead's up to us,' said another.

'It depends how much you're worth to us alive.'

'Nothing,' said Rhiannon.

'Everyone's worth something, my dear.'

'But I've got no money!'

The men shook their heads.

'Such a pretty face,' said one.

'It seems a pity,' said another.

'You'd better come with us anyway,' said a third.

'We'll take you to Agga.'

'Let Agga decide.'

Having no choice Rhiannon went with them up into the mountains, a stony path to some unimaginable fate. Soft rain soaked her, dampened her clothes and hung like beads from her hair. And their talk and laughter was all around her, chivalrous and mocking. Somehow she found it hard to think of them as potential murderers. It was almost as if they had some undefinable code of honour that guaranteed her life. But how much would it cost her? she thought bitterly. And how could she pay? Take out a mortgage on her future? Sing for nothing for the rest of her days?

They came to caverns hewn deep into the rock and the men led her inside. Bright rugs were on the floors and the walls were hung with tapestries, and quiet women moved like shadows serving food at tables. Deeper in, Rhiannon saw electrically lit tunnels and heard a generator running. She was not introduced. Awkwardly and apparently forgotten, she stood clutching her guitar while the men sat down to eat.

There was nothing to prevent her leaving, no doors or prison bars. She could have turned in her tracks and walked away. But near to the cave's entrance a young man sat on a three-legged stool with a lute on his lap, and quietly watched her. He was as dark as Arni and his teeth flashed white when he smiled. Rhiannon scowled and hated him. Then, on the floor beside him, she noticed a pair of crutches. He was lame, she thought without much pity. His right leg was shrivelled and twisted and if she ran he would not be able to follow. But an old woman, stirring a pot over an open fire, was watching her too.

'You want some breakfast, girl?'

'No,' Rhiannon said sourly.

'You'll go hungry until supper then.'

'Does it matter?'

'Does it matter, Rudi?' the old woman asked.

The young man smiled again.

'Only to you,' he told Rhiannon.

Softly, sweetly, Rudi played on the lute. But nothing mattered to Rhiannon, not any more. She sat on a stone at the entrance to the cave, her mood as gloomy as the weather. It was a dreary, dreary planet . . . grey rain over grey mountains and the marshes beneath her wreathed in mist. And Arni had left her there, sold her, not caring how she was used or if she were alive or dead. The porridge grew cold in a porcelain dish and she could not even taste it.

It was her own fault really.

It was her own fault for trying to compete. But she had not meant it that way. Every song she had sung had been for Arni and the only prize she had ever wanted was the congratulations of his smile. And would it have made any difference if he had known that? Somehow she doubted it. Arni only had one desire and that was to win. And the desire to win did not bring out the best in people, it was simply a desire to make losers of everyone else, get rid of them as rivals, see them beaten, see them fail. As her mother had said . . . the Song Contest on Penda was nothing to do with art or music. It was just a vicious competition, corrupted by all the incentives . . . gold medallions and the minstrel's crown, applause, acclaim and triumph, jealousy and spite and the accolade of audiences, fortune and fame. It had turned Arni from a possible human being into an unscrupulous fiend. And if Rhiannon ever competed again her only motive would be revenge, a desire to see Arni the loser and herself the winner, as ruthless as he was, a singer with no soul.

'He's not worth it,' the old woman said.

'Who isn't?' asked Rhiannon.

'That young man of yours. He's not worth brooding about.'

'He's *not* my young man!'

'But you came here for him, didn't you?'

'I came for myself,' said Rhiannon.

'Why?' Rudi asked pointedly.

'I was looking for a song, if you must know. And what business is it of yours?'

Rudi shrugged.

'I can sell you a song if you're willing to pay.'

'I've already said I don't have any money.'

'But your father does,' the old woman prompted. 'Or is it your mother? You are obviously one of a kind with that young man and it costs a bit to run your own ship. You come from a rich home, do you? A nice mansion in the posh part of the galaxy?'

'Actually I live on a star cruiser,' Rhiannon said.

'A star cruiser!' exclaimed the old woman. 'Now there's a thing. Which one would that be, my dear?'

There was silence in the cavern, the men watching and listening as the old woman questioned, smiling in anticipation. They were outlaws, thought Rhiannon, as greedy for gold as Arni was for glory. If they knew she was the daughter of a star ship's captain they would probably ask a million dollars or more for her release. And would her mother pay?

'Don't come crying to me if you end up in trouble,' she had said. Remembering, Rhiannon bit her lip.

'My father cleans the cabins,' she said.

The men laughed.

'What now, Agga?'

'Shall we throw her over the cliff?'

'Shall we feed her to the marsh eels?'

'Or will you give her to Rudi for a wife?'

Agga turned on them with the ladle in her hand.

'Get out!' she said savagely. 'Get out, the lot of you! I'll deal with this and I don't need no funny remarks! And Rudi has enough to bear without you ragging him!'

Rhiannon watched in astonishment.

The men obeyed.

One by one they shuffled meekly away and vanished into the mountain, or else dissolved outside in the mist and rain. Only the women remained, quietly eating their own meal as Rudi played the lute. His head was bent and he no longer looked at Rhiannon, and the chords were moody, reflecting what he felt. Technically, she noted, he was far from perfect. But his music moved her, his soul in the strings, hurt and sad and full of longing. She wondered if he could sing as well as he played, if his voice had that same extraordinary quality of expression. But Agga's harsh voice interrupted her thoughts.

'Play something lively,' she commanded.

'Maybe he doesn't want to,' Rhiannon said.

Rudi put down the lute and reached for his crutches. He was tall when he stood.

'I can speak for myself!' he said harshly. 'I don't need protecting any more than you do, apparently, although you must have been mad or stupid to come here. And even more stupid following *him*! He sold you to us without batting an eyelid and now we're going to take you for every penny you've got. Because in the end that's all that matters, isn't it? That's what you sing for, and he sings for, and everyone sings for, as if there's nothing else in the whole damned universe except money. And don't give me that crap about cleaning cabins! You're loaded, lady, just like he was!'

Agga cackled as he limped from the cave.

Then rubbed her hands.

Her old voice cooed at Rhiannon.

'Shall we say a hundred thousand dollars, my dear?'

*

Rhiannon sat on a ledge of rock. She had spent every penny she had ever won on buying her ship, but Agga would not believe her. Quite simply, if she wanted to leave Taska she had to pay. For a hundred thousand dollars they would contact the star cruiser and ask for her to be collected, or send for the space rescue service to repair her ship. If not, she could stay, work with the rest of the women grubbing a living from the land.

Wet, grey and uninviting the planet lay before her, hundreds and thousands of kilometers of mountain and bog, carnivorous marsh eels and unseen birds screaming in the clouds above. It was a dismal prospect. She had been a nomad all her life and could not bear to be permanently grounded. It was like losing her sight or her hearing, a terrible disablement. Already the grey clouds stifled her and she longed to be moving among space and stars. Tears of misery trickled down her face.

And who cared, she thought. Who cared about her? She was alone and friendless, alienated from everyone, even from her own mother. Ebo, Denny, her mother and father . . . all she had ever done was use people to get where she wanted. A child with a dream, a girl loving Arni, she had competed as ruthlessly as he had, wanting to win for her own selfish reasons. And now she had lost, everything and everyone. Nothing remained but the mist and the rain and shambling footsteps dislodging the stones behind her.

'I've brought your guitar,' said Rudi.

'What for?' Rhiannon asked crossly. 'There's no point in my playing that any more.'

'I find it helps,' said Rudi.

'How?' Rhiannon asked him.

'Whenever I feel down I play the lute, then I feel better. Music's like sunlight, it lifts the spirit.'

'I've not noticed,' Rhiannon retorted.

Gently he laid it on the edge of the rock.

And awkwardly he sat beside her.

'I've always wanted a Banjulian guitar,' he said.

'Then you may as well have it,' Rhiannon told him.

'Does it mean so little that you'll give it away?'

'Stuck here, it means nothing at all!'

'Stuck here,' said Rudi, 'it's all I have and all I'm ever likely to have. Without my lute I think I wouldn't want to live.'

'So why do you stay here?' Rhiannon muttered.

He spread his hands.

'I'm a cripple,' he said simply.

Rhiannon bit her lip.

'I'm sorry.'

'Who for?' asked Rudi. 'Me or yourself?'

She shrugged.

She was sorry for herself, of course, and she had not really thought about him. But it seemed he was as much a prisoner on Taska as she was and the planet trapped them both. And even if he was not a cripple there was no way off, Rudi told her. She frowned and looked at him then.

'But you're outlaws,' Rhiannon said. 'You can do what you like and go where you like and no one can stop you.'

Rudi laughed, but not at her.

It was bitter, mocking laughter.

They had been miners once, he said, employed by the Galactic Mining Company, working long hours for low wages that a few unknown men might grow rich. Then they had gone on strike, demanded improved conditions and a share of the profits. So the Company had pulled out, had them declared outlaws by the judicial courts, and left them stranded. They had no ship of their own, and even if they had there was no one capable of piloting it.

'It's a penal colony,' said Rudi. 'We run it ourselves but it's still a penal colony. I was born here and my parents died here, and when I got ill there wasn't even a medic. Polio, Agga said it was. It left me paralysed but there were other children who didn't recover.'

'I'm sorry,' Rhiannon said again.

Rudi shrugged.

'I'm used to it,' he said.

It was horrible, thought Rhiannon, a horrible place
. . . mist and rain and an almost sunless climate . . . and
nothing to eat but porridge and whortle berries and
marsh-eel stew. They traded with gypsies, Rudi told her.
Porcelain dishes and coloured clothes to brighten their
lives. And they gained an income from whoever happened to land there . . . speculators, adventurers,
unwary travellers, Arni and Rhiannon. And there was
no way off, not until they could afford to charter a space
ship, hire lawyers and barristers and return to the courts
to take on the Company and clear their names.

'And what about you?' asked Rudi.

'What about me?' Rhiannon muttered.

'Your life,' said Rudi.

'I don't want to talk about it,' Rhiannon said. 'Because
it's over, isn't it? I'm stuck here on Taska, with you.'

'You can't really expect us to believe you're poor,' said
Rudi.

'All I've got is a credit card, about five hundred dollars
in a bank account and my Banjulian guitar,' said
Rhiannon.

Rudi frowned.

'I think you're in trouble,' he said.

'Unless you help me,' said Rhiannon.

There was a small silence.

Rainwater trickled between the stones.

And in the cave behind them a woman sang.

'How?' asked Rudi.

'Agga seems fond of you,' said Rhiannon.

'She's my grandmother,' said Rudi.

'So if you could persuade her . . .'

'I could try, I suppose.'

'I'd be no use on Taska anyway,' said Rhiannon. 'And
my parents are just employees of a company. There's no
way they could pay a hundred thousand dollars for my
release. All I need is a single radio message, a few simple

repairs to my ship. And Arni's already paid for that. So what's the point in keeping me here? I mean . . . if you're not going to murder me, you might as well let me go.'

'I'll see what I can do,' said Rudi.

'Now?' asked Rhiannon.

'Later,' said Rudi. 'I'll pick my moment.'

It was something to hope for and Rhiannon was inclined not to push him into taking immediate action. She was too aware that she was using him, just as she had used Ebo and her mother, for her own ends. And if everything worked out she would leave without a backward glance, return to the stars and the Song Contest on Penda with no regrets and nothing lost but her time. Not even that . . . for in the cave behind her a woman sang.

Rhiannon turned her head.

The voice was sweet and lilting.

But she was too far away to hear the words.

'Do you know that song?' she asked Rudi.

'It's a traditional ballad,' he told her.

'How does it go? Show me.'

Rudi picked up the guitar, strummed uncertainly and searched for the chords, humming the same tune. Rhiannon waited, watched impatiently, then took it from him and began to play.

'Just sing,' she told him.

And nothing mattered after that, nothing but the music flowing through her and the song Rudi sang, the tone of his voice, the meaning, the words. Sheer delight welled up inside her. It was beautiful, the most beautiful song she had ever heard. Trapped on a grey wet world among a band of outlaws, she had found what she had always dreamed of . . . a love song for Arni.

Her eyes shone at the end of it.

'That was wonderful,' she said.

And she would learn it, she thought, sing it for Arni although she no longer loved him, or even cared. She would sing it to match him, outmatch him, beat him, defeat him, make him a loser and take away his minstrel's crown. She would sing it knowing every word would destroy him, and his humiliation would be her revenge. That was the meaning of competition, the twisted unhealthy feelings of winning and losing, triumph and failure, a corruption of everyone's desire to excel. But the song was incorruptible, poetry and music, and beautiful always no matter who sang it. And who could sing it better than Rudi? Rhiannon thought. Not she, nor Arni of Goth.

The rain had stopped. Pale sunlight filtered through the clouds and she could see the silver gleam of her ship in the marshes beneath. Crippled, she thought, just like Rudi. And so was she . . . crippled by her own ambition, concerned with nothing else. It was as if she had learned nothing from all her years of experience. And what was the point? she thought. What was the point of winning if she lost her ability to acknowledge the worth of another, her human caring, her own soul? She had lost already . . . love and affection and friendship . . . Ebo and her mother, disregarded and cast aside. Now, would she do the same with Rudi, who was willing to help her, persuade Agga to let her go without a thought for himself?

She glanced at him.

A song belonged to anyone and she had no right to claim it for herself and reap the rewards. It would be sheer selfishness if she did and she did not want to be that way, following Arni, not any more. But could she give up her own chance of winning and let Rudi win instead? Be glad for him as she had once been glad for Arni and find joy in his success? She placed the guitar on his lap.

'Take it,' she said.

'What for?' he asked her.

'I'll teach you to play,' she said. 'And how would you like to come with me, leave Taska behind and sing in the Song Contest on Penda?'

Rudi stared at her.

He was dark, like Arni.

And his teeth flashed white as he smiled.

4

The Death Flower

Binary suns shone through the arched windows of the great Academy, filled the halls and corridors with double shadows and diffuse light. Students thronged the main staircase, heading down through misty yellow air as Ky elbowed his way up. A marble bannister was cool to his touch and with each turn of the stair his excitement grew. Conversations faded below him, filtered away into silences of laboratories and lecture rooms, and he walked alone along the high corridor to the Principal's office. It was very quiet in that part of the building. Every small sound seemed magnified . . . the scuff of his shoes on polished stone, the trill of a phone in a closed room, and distant voices. Recognizing them, Ky stopped walking. The door was ajar and their words were clear, and he eavesdropped on an argument about himself.

'I would prefer not to take a student along on this particular trip,' Hal Arrison said.

'Ky was assigned to you months ago!' the Principal retorted.

'Maybe next time . . .'

'We can't reshuffle the whole academic schedule at a moment's notice!'

'Dr Largo particularly requested . . .'

'Who's Dr Largo?'

'He's a botanist employed by the Galactic Council.'

'And you expect me to deny one of my students essential off-world experience because some plant buff wants to walk unwitnessed through the planetary flora? Why can't he find another ship?'

'At the moment they're all out on contract.'

'And you're under contract to this Academy!'

'You don't understand,' Hal-Arrison said impatiently. 'It's official business and I've been commandeered.'

'Well, I've not been notified,' said the Principal.

There was a small silence.

'Okay,' Hal-Arrison said quietly. 'So it's unofficial. But I've two X-rated planets on my list and it's no routine mission. I can only repeat . . . I would prefer not to take a student along on this particular trip.'

'I'm sure Ky can handle it,' replied the Principal.

And that seemed like an appropriate moment.

Ky knocked at the door and entered.

'You sent for me, sir?'

Hal-Arrison was no stranger. Attached to the Academy, Ky had seen him many times before laughing and talking with various groups of students in the briefing room, or striding the corridors in his navy blue flying suit. But they had never actually met. Now, being introduced to him, Ky held out his hand. Binary suns shone through the arched window . . . and he was a golden man, tall and blond, everyone's hero turning towards him. Violet eyes fixed on Ky's face but he did not smile. One cold curt nod was all Hal-Arrison gave to the boy who would accompany him to other worlds among the stars.

'Are you packed and ready?' asked the Principal.

'Yes,' said Ky.

'Good,' said the Principal studying the flight schedule. 'You'll be leaving from Bay Eleven. There will be a Dr Largo travelling with you and the planets listed are X21 and X33.'

'We've already studied X33,' said Ky.

'Excellent,' said the Principal. 'Forewarned is forearmed then. Take-off is at 09.00 hours and the transit shuttle leaves at 06.30. Have a good trip. And please remember to behave at all times in accordance with your training. Is there anything you wish to add, Hal-Arrison?'

The survey pilot spread his hands.

His violet eyes softened as he made his appeal.

'Don't come with me,' he said.

The Principal rose from his chair.

'It's not Ky's choice to make!' he said angrily.

Ky was sent away to wait in the library and this time he heard nothing of what was said, nor could he guess what the final outcome would be. And useless to wonder why, truly, Hal-Arrison did not want to take him. Students had visited X-rated planets before, X33 in particular, although Ky knew nothing of X21. And the library computer contained scant information . . . just its size, position, atmospheric and climatic conditions and the main topographical features. It was simply another classified planet, isolated in a limb of the galaxy, with no embassy, no exchange of trade or culture, and where all unauthorized landings were forbidden. No reason was given for that. The inhabitants were listed as humanoid and intellectually advanced. Ky supposed they must be hostile, as they were on X33, clever people locked into a lower level of consciousness. But maybe he would never really know.

'Don't come with me,' Hal-Arrison had said.

And already an hour had gone by.

Then the door opened softly.

'Are you Ky?' asked the Principal's secretary.

'Yes,' he told her.

'Then it's all systems go,' she said.

Ky passed through the boarding gates of the orbiting space station to where the small ship waited, silver-bright against a backdrop of space and stars. Hal-Arrison accepted him with a shrug, silently stowed away his luggage and led him on board. Already seated and strapped down ready for take-off was a portly middle-aged man with a balding head. Dr Largo, Ky supposed, although in his white jungle outfit of shorts and shirt he looked more like a big-game hunter than a botanist, and there was a small primitive revolver in a leather holster around his waist. Pale eyes glinted coldly behind a pair of spectacles.

'So this is our student?' he said.

'Ky,' Hal-Arrison said curtly.

Dr Largo smiled.

But his eyes stayed cold.

And he cracked his knuckles.

'Who knows, he may be of use to us,' he said.

'Just leave him out of it!' Hal-Arrison snapped.

Ky felt a trickle of unease, a tensing of nerves in his stomach like sickness or fear, but seated beside Hal-Arrison in the cockpit he instantly forgot. Deft fingers flicked the controls and the hangar doors opened automatically as the ship eased its way out. Ky watched intently, waited to be instructed, but Hal-Arrison made no attempt. He just set the flight path, increased speed and made the jump into hyper-space without a word. Violet eyes brooded as stars streaked past the windows and Ky might not have been there. Not until they slowed to approach the first planet did Hal-Arrison finally speak.

'Merion,' he murmured.

'I thought we were heading for X21,' said Ky.

'Merion *is* X21,' Hal-Arrison replied.

'You know it, then?'

'We do an aerial survey every few years.'

Under the pale light of a nearby sun a planet slowly revolved, a world of brown land and grey water, continents and seas, and cloud banks drifting through the atmosphere. It was nothing like the flight simulator on which Ky had practised. This planet was real. Not holograms and a laser light and an exit back into the Academy, but an alien landfall coming closer as the ship went down.

'Keep a look-out,' Hal-Arrison told him.

'What for?' asked Ky.

'You'll know if you see it,' the pilot replied.

Clouds obscured his view. Then they emerged and below was a landscape of rolling hills and dead vegetation, a forest perhaps, dry, brown and leafless. Deciduous, thought Ky, in the middle of the winter season. But he saw no evidence of frost or snow. For hundreds of miles the jungle went on, brown matted colour broken only by the silver shine of rivers, sunlight and shadows drifting across it. Nothing was alive on this part of Merion . . . not a bird, not a flower, not a blade of grass, nor any signs of human settlement.

'Do you see anything?'

Unheard Dr Largo had entered the cockpit.

His pale eyes peered through the windows.

And his knuckles cracked.

'It's just like I told you,' Hal-Arrison said.

But Ky saw something on the land beneath the undergrowth. He saw perhaps shapes of fields, bare earth sucked clean of sustenance, a few ruined buildings, then fallen walls and a pattern of streets.

'There's a ruined city down there,' he said.

'Very likely,' Hal-Arrison muttered.

'What happened to it?'

'What do you think happened?'

'Atomic war?' suggested Ky.

'Just war,' Hal-Arrison said darkly. 'And poverty and pollution, the mass slaughter of animals for food, rape and murder and violence . . . whatever else is acceptable in an unenlightened civilization. They never reached the atomic stage on Merion.'

His voice was scathing. And he might have been talking of X33, thought Ky, although it had recently gone atomic. Decadent and unstable, X33 was a prime example of a renegade civilization. At the Academy it was part of the curriculum and what to do about it became every student's problem. Left alone it would either run out of resources, be polluted to the point where it could no longer support life, blow itself up or else turn its attention outwards, conquering and destroying other worlds in other solar systems. And whatever happened, everyone agreed that sooner or later the Galactic Council would be forced to act.

'Have they made up their minds about X33?' asked Ky.

'Who?' Hal-Arrison asked sharply.

'The Galactic Council,' said Ky.

Dr Largo cracked his knuckles.

His eyes gleamed strangely.

And his voice was soft, almost menacing.

'I'd advise you not to ask questions, boy.'

Hal-Arrison laughed mockingly.

'He's a student,' he said. 'What the hell else do you expect him to do?'

Ky felt silent.

It was true, he thought, all he had overheard in the Principal's office. This was no routine mission and Dr Largo was no ordinary botanist. He was employed by the Galactic Council and the trip to Merion was directly connected with the fate of X33. Commandeered, Hal-Arrison said. And unofficially Ky had become involved.

For many hours Hal-Arrison's ship flew above the land searching for something Ky never saw. It must be a plant, he supposed, for Dr Largo seemed not much interested in the human inhabitants of the planet, the broken remains of a former civilization and those who had survived in the white walled towns along the sea coast and the villages further north. Where the land grew green and wooded among lakes and mountains, and fields grew summer crops, he had Hal-Arrison turn south again towards the jungle.

Its deadness, Ky learned, had nothing to do with latitude or season. It had been dead for the last hundred years or more, Dr Largo said, but he wanted to be sure. And the brown monotony of tangled undergrowth remained beneath them, lifeless and unchanging, through noon and afternoon and into evening. Only at sunset when the hills burned orange and the valleys deepened with umber shade and the sky and land blazed with fiery colours, was it briefly beautiful. But by then Ky was too tired to care. His eyes ached from looking, and his body ached from sitting, and his stomach curdled with emptiness. He had had nothing to eat since leaving the Academy except protein cubes and glucose tablets.

'It's getting too dark to see,' Hal-Arrison complained.

'So what do you suggest?' inquired Dr Largo.

'It's not up to me, is it?'

'I suppose we must land then.'

'Anywhere in particular?' Hal-Arrison asked.

'I leave it to you,' replied Dr Largo.

They touched down softly, twenty minutes later, on silvery sand at the edge of a lake. The cruise motors cut into a shock of silence, but the noise and vibrations continued to roar in Ky's head and he made no attempt to move. Physically, mentally and emotionally, he felt shattered. And, as if he understood, Hal-Arrison leaned across him, pulled the handle and opened the emergency door. 'You need to acclimatize,' Hal-Arrison said.

Soft air brushed Ky's face, resinous and warm. And as the vibrations faded and the world settled and stilled, he saw trees growing on a nearby promontory and lights of a settlement gleaming beyond. And after a while he began to distinguish sounds . . . lake water lapping, the sigh of the wind, a small bird twittering and the loud crack of a twig.

'Dr Largo is busy already,' Hal-Arrison remarked.

'So what's he looking for?' asked Ky.

'That's not for me to say.'

Hal-Arrison yawned and rose from his seat and left the cockpit. Ky heard voices softly talking, things being unloaded from the ship's storage compartment, the rattle of cutlery. Twilight deepened and a pale moon rose

81

above the lake and he could have stayed there all night, peaceful and sleepy. Then he smelled food . . . hot soup and protein cutlets frying . . . and on the strange heavy earth of Merion, Ky finally set foot, tottered on shaky legs across the few metres of sand to claim his supper.

'Ah,' said Dr Largo. 'It's our student.'

'Ky,' said Hal-Arrison. 'His name's Ky.'

'In botany,' said Dr Largo, 'we don't recognize individuals, only species. To my way of thinking a flower is a flower, and a student is a student. They're all the same to me.'

'And bullshit is bullshit!' Hal-Arrison responded.

Cross-legged on the ground, under a night sky blazing with unknown stars, the two men ate and argued and Ky listened. They did not like each other, he decided. There were cross-currents of feelings and edges to their words, barbed insinuations he did not understand and meanings that were not quite clear. But something was going on which Hal-Arrison did not agree with; something to do with Dr Largo's attitude and the undefined purpose of the trip. And what was it here on Merion that Dr Largo wanted but Hal-Arrison did not?

Ky glanced around, his senses sharpened. Small sounds of life were everywhere — night songs of birds and insects and some small creature scuttling through the dry edge of grass. But only the lake margins lived. Beyond and behind him was an eerie stillness, an absolute silence where the jungle began. It was dead, thought Ky, a dead silence. Or maybe not. He peered and listened and his flesh crawled and fear lurched in his stomach. Something was alive out there in the tangled darkness, something terrible and formless, watching and waiting and knowing he was there.

'Can you feel her?' Dr Largo said softly.

Ky turned his head.

Moonlight shone on a pair of spectacles.

And his knuckles cracked.

And his teeth showed white as he smiled.

'Can you feel her, boy?'

'What is it?' Ky asked fearfully.

'She is the death flower,' the little man breathed. 'The soul of her lives. But her thorns sleep until we wake her . . . then she tears your flesh from your bones.'

'I told you not to come on this trip,' Hal-Arrison said.

Ky dreamed nightmares, woke with a cry and instantly forgot. It was morning on Merion . . . trees on the promontory silhouetted against the sunrise and pale smoke rising from the village beyond. Snug in his sleeping bag on soft sand, he lay listening to the lake water lapping the shore. But then he remembered the death flower and turned to look.

In daylight she was not so impressive, just mounds of dead brambles and black earth beneath. Perfectly harmless, Hal-Arrison had assured him, providing they left her alone. But now Hal-Arrison was sleeping and along the jungle's edge Dr Largo had begun his search.

Curious, Ky crawled from his sleeping bag. Once upon a time, Dr Largo had told him, the death flower had been green and blooming over most of the planet, but now only her thorns remained and her dark seeds buried. She needed blood in order to germinate, emotional terror, some blundering creature to impale itself on her spikes. But the people of Merion were aware of her habits and had altered their natures to defy her, and animals avoided her instinctively. Now, on barbs long as a hand span, only the spiders built their webs, gossamer threads hung with drops of dew that shivered and sparkled in the wind and sun. Perfectly harmless, thought Ky. But Dr Largo poked at her roots with a stick.

'What are you looking for?' Ky asked him.

'Seeds,' puffed Dr Largo.

'What do you need seeds for?'

'To sow,' said Dr Largo. 'What else?'

'Isn't that dangerous?' asked Ky.

'I'm a botanist,' said Dr Largo. 'To me this is simply

83

another plant. And don't just stand there, boy. Come and give me a hand.'

Ky fetched a length of driftwood from the shore and returned to join him, digging in earth and shadows and the scent of rotting leaves. Dry thorns snapped and blue-black beetles scuttled for cover. He found worms and a chrysalid and a nest of flying ants, but nothing that looked like a seed. And Dr Largo watched him expectantly, his pale eyes gleaming, leaf-mould clinging to his clothes. They would have to dig deeper, he said, deeper and further in. Discard their sticks and use their hands perhaps? And he would return to the ship and find a shovel. Ky squatted. The soil was rich and sweet beneath his fingers, and the death flower waited with her arms full of thorns.

Then, quite suddenly, someone pushed him and he lost his balance, toppled forwards and fell to his knees . . . and a thorn raked his hand. He knew a moment of fear, saw blood and darkness and the seeds of the death flower moving in the earth. They were winged like insects, about to take flight. Or maybe they were ants? Ky was not sure. He just cried out in terror, beat them away, and thorns hooked in his hair. He screamed then . . . and Dr Largo stood there, watching and smiling and not attempting to help.

It was Hal-Arrison who came to Ky's assistance, dragged him free, hauled him to his feet and slapped him hard around the face. The shock made a stillness inside him. Stunned, Ky stared into the violet eyes that stared into his own. The pilot's hands were firm on his shoulders and his voice was soft, almost hypnotic.

'Don't move!' Hal-Arrison said. 'Stay right where you are, absolutely quiet and still. Hang on to yourself and don't think about anything. Now, concentrate on your breathing. Deep breaths, deep and slow. Feel your heartbeats quieten. That's good. That's very good. Keep those deep breaths coming.'

'You fool,' Dr Largo said softly.

Hal-Arrison ignored him.

He went on talking to Ky.

'Don't listen,' he said. 'Don't listen to him or look behind you. I'm sorry I hit you but everything is going to be all right. There's nothing to fear. Remember that. Now, I want you to walk very slowly towards the ship. Walk, don't run. I'll come with you.'

Gripping Ky's arm Hal-Arrison led him forward. The sand was soft and sunlight rippled on the water and small birds fluted among the reeds. There was nothing to fear, Hal-Arrison said. Three steps up and the hatch closed behind them with a thud. He was safe now, thought Ky. But his face burned, and his head dripped blood, and violet fury blazed in Hal-Arrison's eyes.

'I told you to stay away from that thing!'

'Dr Largo asked me . . .'

'So stay away from him too!'

'I don't understand!' cried Ky. 'What happened?'

Hal-Arrison reached for the first-aid tin.

'She's sensate!' he snapped. 'A sensate plant! She's aware of your emotions and fear attracts her. That's what happened to the civilization on Merion. She fed on it! She fed on all the stupidity and wrongness and wretchedness until no one was left but the wise. And *he* wants to revive her. He wants to bring the death flower back to life. So stay away from him. Right?'

Iodine on the scratch made Ky yelp and his eyes watered as he stared through the window. Outside Dr Largo squatted, raked through the soil for the seeds he had almost had, a plump little man in white shorts and a sun hat, not caring how much it cost in blood or life. It was the species that mattered, not individuals, he had said. And if it had not been for Hal-Arrison's intervention Ky might be dead by now, a victim of the death flower returning to life.

He bit his lip.

'Dr Largo pushed me,' he said bitterly.

'What?' said Hal-Arrison. 'Are you sure?'

'I felt a hand against my back,' said Ky. 'And who else was there?'

Hal-Arrison gave him antiseptic cream and a sticking plaster.

'Stay here,' he said. 'I want a word with our Dr Largo.'

Ky watched from the window. The ship was sound-proofed and he could not hear what the two men said but they appeared to be having an argument. Anger was plain on Hal-Arrison's face and Dr Largo stamped his foot impatiently. Ky chewed a protein cube and waited, and time on the control console ticked twenty minutes away. Then Hal-Arrison returned. They were going to the village, he said, and it might be a good idea if Ky stayed there.

'I can pick you up on the way back,' Hal-Arrison said.

'You mean you'll go to X33 and leave me here?'

'You'll be quite safe . . . the natives are friendly.'

'What about my academic schedule?'

'It's better to miss out on planetary experience than the rest of your life,' Hal-Arrison informed him.

Ky stared at him in disbelief, then stared through the window to where Dr Largo waited. Sunlight glinted on his spectacles and he carried a revolver at his belt.

'He wouldn't!' said Ky.

'I don't trust him,' Hal-Arrison said darkly.

'But that would be murder!'

'And I'm responsible for your safety.'

'He's employed by the Galactic Council!'

'Exactly,' Hal-Arrison said grimly.

'You mean *they* would condone it?'

'Just pack your bag,' Hal-Arrison said.

The plaster on Ky's hand smelled sweetly of medi-cation and he packed hurriedly, trying to understand what he knew. The Galactic Council ruled over the whole Federation of Planets, great men gathered together, representatives of worlds. Their purpose was to protect individuals and ensure the essential freedoms of all life forms. He could not believe they would sanction anything unlawful. Hal-Arrison was wrong, thought Ky, and he must have been mistaken to think Dr Largo pushed him. He was just a botanist, employed by the Galactic Council, and eminently respectable. Plump, smiling, he came to the foot of the steps.

'I hear you're leaving us,' he said.

'It's not my decision,' Ky retorted.

'You shouldn't have come anyway,' Hal-Arrison snapped.

'Did I have any choice?'

'We all have choice,' said Dr Largo. 'We can obey or not obey . . . others or our own impulses. The capacity for conscious decision making is what distinguishes us from animals, I believe.'

'But in this case *I* make the decisions,' Hal-Arrison said.

Taking Ky's travel bag he strode towards the promontory. Just for a moment Ky felt rebellious, but orders were orders and he had been brought up to obey . . . his parents, his teachers, the rules of society, his whole life geared to accepting authority. Disobedience meant trouble, he had learned. But if he obeyed Hal-Arrison he would miss the rest of the trip. And Dr Largo watched him, studied his reactions, as if he were a specimen. Ky shrugged and headed for the trees. And the botanist followed along a path through dry grass where shade and sunlight flickered.

'Merion, in parts, is very like X33,' he said.

'Is it?' Ky said indifferently.

'Such a beautiful planet,' Dr Largo continued. 'A pity you won't be seeing it. The seas are turquoise, you know, when viewed from a space craft. And the flora is magnificent, a multitude of species and variations of species . . .'

'Yes,' Ky said harshly. 'I *do* know. We've studied it at the Academy. The seas are polluted and species are vanishing. The damage to the environment is almost beyond redemption and the whole planet is inhabited by morons. I prefer to stay on Merion!'

And maybe he did.

Meadows were green beyond the promontory and white walled houses nestled where a river joined the lake. Out on the still water men fished from small boats, and nearer a herd of long-legged shaggy cattle grazed on the lush grass. And there was a girl talking to Hal-Arrison. Even at a distance Ky thought her attractive with her long dark hair, her white embroidered blouse and scarlet skirt. Then, as he approached, her dark eyes fixed on him and a smile lit her features, and she was the first truly beautiful thing he had seen on the drab world of Merion.

'This is Celise,' Hal-Arrison said.

She held out her hands to greet them, Ky and Dr Largo, repeating their names in order to remember. Bright coloured bangles gilded with gold jangled on her arms, and her red skirt swirled, and her blouse was embroidered with claws and feathers, or maybe it was thorns and flowers. There was no hint of nervousness in her manner. Although they were strangers come from another world she simply accepted them.

'You will be welcome to stay in Ben Utha's house,' she told Ky.

'Who's Ben Utha?' he asked her.

'My grandfather,' she said.

'One of the village elders,' said Hal-Arrison.

'You can stay as long as you like,' said Celise.

'Thank you,' Ky said solemnly.

Dr Largo smiled and cracked his knuckles.

'How perfectly charming,' he murmured.

But he did not really feel it, thought Ky.

To him Celise was just another specimen.

And all he wanted were the seeds of the death flower.

Celise led them to a house built beside the lake and in through an archway. Rooms opened on to a central courtyard where a pool of brown water glittered in the sun and massed flowers grew beneath the shade of trees. They each had their own private quarters, Celise explained, but mostly they lived communally, an extended family sharing the chores and the facilities and the children. But Ben Utha came alone to greet them, an old man in white robes, grey-haired and thin, his black eyes shining with life.

'This is my grandfather,' said Celise. 'And this is Ky, Hal-Arrison and Dr Largo who have come from the Federation of Planets.'

Ben Utha smiled and nodded.

'Is all well with our world?' he asked Hal-Arrison.

'For now,' Hal-Arrison replied.

'You are suggesting it will not always be so?'

'We come with a request from the Galactic Council,' Hal-Arrison said.

'Then enter,' Ben Utha said gently. 'And let us discuss it.'

What waited for Ky inside Ben Utha's house was a culture shock. Everything stunned him . . . the incredible richness of colour and design, the patterns that swirled in the fabrics and floor mosaics, on the carved columns and ceiling arches. He was surrounded by sheer art, everything hand-fashioned and exquisite. And dark native people moved around him in their bright embroidered clothes . . . vivid backgrounds of blue and turquoise, green and yellow, and the same swirling pattern being repeated in a riot of silks. Everywhere he looked he was bombarded by colour, by leaves and petals and tangled branches, or maybe it was feathers and claws. He could not be sure. It was all so abstract and undefined.

Like one in a dream he sat at the dark wooden table laden with bread and fish and fruit. And there it was again, inlaid with coloured marquetry, that same strange abstract pattern. And again on the plates and bowls and eating utensils, woven into the linen napkins, engraved on the fire surround and in the gold ring Ben Utha wore on his finger. Ky heard nothing of the conversation. The inflexions of voices were simply a background hum as he sat and gazed. Crystal wind chimes fluttered like birds by an open window making a sweet tinkling music, and somewhere in a schoolroom he heard children singing. But it was all far away, dissolving as the sunlight flickered among the room's colours, over shapes of things and people's faces.

'You're not eating,' Celise remarked.

'No,' murmured Ky.

'Don't you like our food?'

'It's all too much.'

'But you've not eaten anything yet.'

'I mean this,' said Ky, nodding at the room. 'And this,' he said as he touched a porcelain bowl. 'And the pattern in the curtains. And your beads and your bangles and your blouse top. And the tiles on the floor. Did you make it all?'

Celise smiled.

'It made us,' she told him.

'I don't understand.'

'I'll show you,' she offered.

Begging leave of Ben Utha, Celise led him from the house, out through the archway and along the village street. Workrooms opened on to the pavements and displayed the processes involved in making things . . . carpets and lace, fabrics and pottery . . . everywhere the same confusion of movement and pattern and colour. Smells filled the air of plant dyes and sawdust and resin, fire in the forge and molten metal. There were sounds of hammering and chiselling and the rattle of a printing press, shapes being formed out of wood and wrought-iron and paper, fluted lanterns, hanging baskets and carved storage chests, and books with illuminated pages. Everything dazzled, endowed with the life of its maker, unique and beautiful. On everyday objects hands bestowed a value beyond price. Ky saw shirt buttons worth more than diamonds and painted clay beads richer than gold. He touched in reverence, a hair comb fashioned out of water reeds and glue, hardened and set with tiny painted seeds bright as jewels, wondered at all the hours of skill and patience that had gone into making it.

'You want?' asked the woman.

'I didn't bring any money,' said Ky.

'I give,' said the woman.

'I couldn't possibly!'

'If you like what I make it is my honour.'

Ky shook his head.

It was too much to accept.

But Celise picked it up.

'He doesn't understand,' she said. 'His ways are different from ours, I expect. But I'll take it, if I may. And thank you . . . it's very beautiful.'

The woman smiled and nodded.

And Celise fixed the comb in her hair and walked away.

Ky followed.

'You mean you don't have to pay for things on Merion?'

'To admire is to be given,' Celise explained. 'And what other reason is there for making things? To see and want and not be able to have, is the root of discontentment, we are told. It gives rise to greed and jealousy and all manner of bad feelings, and we are not like that on Merion any more.'

Free, thought Ky, everything was free. And the planet was X-rated not because it was dangerous but to protect it from itself. Without landing controls its hospitality would be abused, art works and artifacts grabbed by galactic traders and unscrupulous tourists, sold for immense profits throughout the Federation. Ky himself could leave there a rich man. All he had to do was ask and it would be given . . . a jewelled necklace, a fine china vase, a buckle mounted with pearls. The thought tempted . . . until he entered the village temple.

'There,' said Celise. 'Now do you see?'

She was everywhere, clear and defined, carved in relief on all the columns and wall friezes, green and scarlet on the floor tiles and tapestries and in the stained-glass windows, tangled and entwined. It was what he had been seeing all morning and not understood. She had died long ago, Dr Largo had said. Yet she was alive in every mind and soul, and in everything they made she was immortalized. Ky stared at the images of the death flower in a kind of horror, at the thorns and leaves and blood-red blossoms. She was everywhere around him and inescapable.

'What happened?' he asked.

On a raised dais at the rear of the building, on a lectern carved with leaves and flowers, was a printed book. Celise turned the pages. It was not about gods or angels, great men or prophets, she said, but ordinary people. The history of Merion and the story of the death flower . . . her voice echoed as she told it and Ky listened.

No one knew where it came from, she said. It might have been blown there on the cosmic winds, its seeds coming from elsewhere in the galaxy. Or it might have evolved on Merion. But it came anyway, set down its roots and grew and spread, not in the wild remote places of the planet but in the towns and cities and populated areas. It was splendid at first, clambering over roofs and walls, a mass of green leaves, and scarlet flowers. But its thorns were deadly. Wounds festered and suppurated. And its growth was menacing. Its roots went deep, creeping through every crack and crevice, seeking the soil beneath walls and streets, smothering and destroying. Neither fire nor poison could kill it. It briefly shrivelled, then sprang up again more vigorous than before. There was no getting rid of it and wherever there were people the death flower thrived.

No one realized she was dependent on their ways. On fear and misery they went on feeding her in the days when men beat their wives and children, and street gangs fought at night, and young girls got raped, and old men got mugged . . . when there were wars and murders and intimidation . . . animal experiments and slaughter houses . . . when governments ruled and most work was hateful and most people lived in uncertainty and dread. Sweet, to the death flower, were all the horrors of the civilization on Merion, and sweetly she bloomed in the fields and the factories, on waste tips and spoil heaps, in ghettos and gardens. Her roots broke through the sewers and gas mains and water supplies, and the pollution got worse, the disease and poverty and slow mass starvation.

'She wiped us out,' said Celise. 'Over two thirds of the population died in a couple of decades. It was a kind of natural selection, I suppose, because those who were left were the ones who learned to adapt. They were meek and accepting, pacifist people who hurt no one and harmed nothing, content with their lot in life. So here we are. Nothing dies now on Merion because of us. Nothing is maimed or tortured or made miserable. The death flower has withered but we are better people, I think.'

Ky stared at her.

'I think you're beautiful,' he said.

She smiled, and he flushed. 'All of you,' he added. 'You're all beautiful people.'

'It's not always easy,' Celise admitted.

'What happens when someone riles you?'

'We try not to mind,' she said. 'What we feel is our own responsibility anyway. We don't have to react or get angry. If we're sensitive to other people's needs and our own responses, then most unpleasantness can usually be avoided.'

'But if someone else is behaving badly, making unjust claims or unacceptable demands, then what do you do?' Ky asked her. 'Do you accept what's unacceptable and allow the injustice to continue? I mean if you don't react how can the other person know they're doing something wrong?'

Celise had no time to answer.

The door burst open and Ben Utha entered the temple. A sudden draught set his white robes fluttering, and he was not immune to anger, it seemed, for all he was old and wise. His expression was grim and his dark eyes flashed and there was a power of determination about him that made Dr Largo look small and ineffectual beside him, and reduced Hal-Arrison to a silent witness. Waving his arms Ben Utha approached, and his voice was loud and commanding.

'Ring the bell, Celise!'

She stared at him in alarm.

'What's happened, Grandfather?'

'Nothing as yet,' Ben Utha said curtly. 'And I prefer to keep it that way. So ring the bell, Celise. I need to summon the elders, everyone in the village of adult status. I must be sure I speak for us all on this.'

Celise obeyed, vanished through a door into a bell tower, as Ky waited and Dr Largo nervously cracked his knuckles. Urgent chimes clanged across the surrounding countryside. And when Celise returned she was told to leave and take Ky with her.

'But what's going on?' asked Ky.

'It is not your business,' Ben Utha said angrily.

'Just go,' Hal-Arrison advised him.

Bewildered, they waited outside. And, summoned by the bell, people were beginning to arrive . . . men from the workshops, women from the houses, farmers from the fields wiping soil from their hands. And down by the quayside fishermen hauled in their nets. Murmuring, questioning, everyone headed for the temple as youths and girls and wide-eyed children stood about and watched. Something was happening in their village, something unusual and important which they were banned from knowing.

'What's it about?' a girl asked Ky.

'I don't know,' he told her.

'Surely it's connected with your visit here?'

'I expect we'll be told later,' said Celise.

'What if we're not?' asked a boy.

'Then we'll never know, will we?'

'We could find out,' said Ky.

'How?' asked the boy.

'There's a window open at the back. I noticed the draught when Ben Utha opened the door.'

They went through a graveyard among long grass and flowers. But the window was high above their heads, the hum of human voices no louder than an angry hum of bees. A group of younger children were despatched to fetch a ladder from the stonemason's yard and they had to take it in turns to listen. It was the little man with glasses, said a girl. He claimed to be authorized by the Galactic Council and was demanding their co-operation. But Ben Utha replied that Merion was independent and self-governing and the Galactic Council had no jurisdiction there. And wherever he went the answer would be the same.

'So what does he want?' asked a boy.

'Whatever it is the village won't give it,' said the girl.

'But we always give what others want,' said Celise.

'Not always,' said the boy.

'Usually,' said Celise.

'It must be too many cream cakes,' said the girl.

'You mean he's being greedy?'

'Hush,' said the boy. 'Let me listen.'

Ky leaned against the white stuccoed wall. There was sunlight on his face and he knew what Dr Largo wanted, a seed of the death flower. But it was only an animal, said a boy, a single shaggy kine from the village herd was what he wanted. One individual from a whole species was no great loss, he was saying, and he could use force if he had to.

'Force?' said Celise.

'He means violence,' said a girl.

'Violence is forbidden!' said another.

'It's against the laws of Merion,' said a third.

'And what does he want with one of our animals?' asked Celise.

Ky felt sick.

Innocent and unknowing, the long-legged cattle grazed quietly in the fields beyond the graveyard, swishing their tails to ward away the flies. And along the horizon the death flower lay like a brown shroud waiting. It would only take one and one individual meant nothing to Dr Largo. He would probably torture it, thought Ky, fill it with fear and kill it slowly, shedding its blood and feeding it to the death flower that her seeds could germinate and spring into life.

Anger rose inside the temple. If he did that, Ben Utha declared, if he used force or inflicted injury on any living thing then they would cripple Hal-Arrison's ship and Dr Largo would be grounded on Merion for the rest of his days. The villagers applauded, shouted their agreement, and outside young eyes widened in astonishment. Threat had been answered by counter-threat and the soft voice of a girl spoke what Ben Utha spoke in the final silence.

'You may dig as you will for the seeds of the death flower but you will use neither bird nor beast nor any sensate thing that lives on Merion to bring her back to life. Here she has had her day and we, who have survived her reign, can wish no other world the same experience. We will not help you seed some other planet! We condemn the decision of the Galactic Council to do so. We condemn you for your willingness to carry it out, Dr Largo. And you for your complicity, Hal-Arrison. Now go. Leave our village and do not come back!'

Inside there was uproar.

Outside the young eyes turned on Ky.

He saw horror on the faces.

He felt their detestation.

'So that's why you're here!' said a boy.

'You've come to kill our cattle!' said a girl.

'And you want to see people die,' said another.

'Millions,' said a boy, 'on some other world.'

'You must be totally soulless,' said a girl.

'You must be completely inhuman!' said a boy.

'It's nothing to do with me!' Ky said wretchedly.

'But you came with them,' said Celise.

'I never knew . . .'

'But you came with them! And you'll leave with them! By association you'll accept what's evil!'

'I've got no choice, have I?'

'That's everyone's excuse!' Celise said coldly.

'It was ours, once,' said a boy.

'But not any more,' said Celise.

She turned on her heel and walked away.

And the others followed her.

In the sunlight of Merion, Ky stood damned and alone.

He was heedless of time, heedless of everything except the thoughts that whirled in his head, a hideous knowledge of what he was involved with. It was what Hal-Arrison had tried to spare him from and failed, every student's problem suddenly become real. And now he was guilty, by association, for a decision made by the Galactic Council without his knowing and the planned genocide of a planet. Dr Largo would drop the seeds of the death flower on X33 and countless millions of people would die.

But they would die anyway, thought Ky, of their own greed and their own stupidity, of over-population, soil erosion, disease, pollution, starvation and war. Genocide was inevitable on X33, but given the death flower some of them might learn, and the survivors would be like the survivors on Merion . . . better people. And was it evil then, what the Galactic Council planned to do? Was it soulless and inhuman? And was it true what Dr Largo believed . . . that it did not really matter what happened to individuals as long as the species survived? The questions confused and troubled him. Between good and evil, wrong and right, it seemed he no longer knew the difference.

Nearby someone coughed politely.

And Ky turned his head.

'I've been looking for you,' said Ben Utha.

'Why?' asked Ky.

'You're my guest, are you not?'

'Where's Hal-Arrison?'

'Returned to the ship.'

'I may as well join him then.'

'Is that your decision?' Ben Utha inquired.

'I can hardly stay here, on Merion, can I? So I'm damned whatever I do.'

The old man smiled.

'Celise is young,' he said gently. 'Young people are apt to speak and act emotionally. They do not always understand another's position or make allowances. Had she obeyed my instructions, of course, and not listened at the window, your little altercation would not have happened and nor would you be burdened by what you know now.'

'I don't know what to do!' Ky said desperately.

'No one can tell another what to do,' Ben Utha said. 'But there is a room in my house, and I shall make you welcome if you choose to stay.'

'Is it right though?' Ky asked him.

'Is what right?'

'Is it right I should stay on Merion? Close my eyes to what goes on and pretend I don't know? A whole planet is going to be devastated! Millions of people are going to die! How can I live with myself if I do nothing?'

Ben Utha rested a comforting hand on his shoulder.

'Listen,' he said. 'The decision made by the Galactic Council was not your decision. And what Hal-Arrison and Dr Largo do is also not your decision. You will not be responsible for bringing the death flower back to life, or for her transportation to this other world. So why must you feel guilty? And what you fear may not happen anyway. They may change their minds or they may dig forever and never find a single seed.'

'But that's not very likely, is it?'

'I would say it's more than likely,' Ben Utha replied. 'In fact, if gambling were not forbidden, I would stake my life on it.'

Ky stared at him.

He felt as though a great dark cloud had been lifted from his mind, as if he had been to a confessional and had his sins forgiven. Whatever happened was not his fault and he could do as he liked, go or stay, without worrying about the consequences. Suddenly Merion was beautiful again, green fields under sunlight where shaggy cattle grazed, white-washed houses and quiet people living quiet lives. The death flower would go on sleeping and they would leave as they had come, without disturbing it. And X33 would suffer a different fate for which, again, Ky would not be responsible.

'Your life?' said Ky.

'My life,' said Ben Utha.

'In that case I'll go back to the ship. I'll help Dr Largo dig for nothing and then we'll leave. And thank you, Ben Utha. Give my regards to Celise.'

The old man nodded.

And he raised his hand in a gesture of farewell.

Ky was half-way across the fields to the promontory when he heard someone calling. Celise, bright as a butterfly in the still heat of the afternoon, came running after him. Her scarlet skirt fluttered and her long hair was falling from its comb . . . and she was carrying the travel bag Ky had forgotten.

'I wanted to apologize,' she said breathlessly.

'Ben Utha did that,' Ky told her.

'And I've brought you a present,' she announced.

'What for?' Ky asked her.

'Take it . . . please.'

It was a beautiful thing she placed in his hand, a small glass paperweight warm from her holding. In its depths transparent swirls of scarlet looked like the petals of a flower and there was a scrap of solider darkness lying at the centre of it. He examined it closely . . . some kind of winged insect, legless and inert. A termite, perhaps?

'Do you like it?' Celise asked anxiously.

'What is it?' he asked her.

'You came here to find it,' she told him. 'It's a seed of the death flower. You can have it to remember us by.'

Ky laughed.

'As if I'm ever likely to forget,' he said softly.

She walked beside him to the promontory. They might never see each other again, she said sadly. And did he really have to go back to the ship? Could he not stay a while with her, the rest of the day, the coming night, throughout tomorrow, however long it took for Hal-Arrison and Dr Largo to give up their search? Why spend his time grubbing in the ground for a seed that would never be found when he could go swimming in the lake, spend the evening singing and dancing and share Ben Utha's supper?

Her smile beguiled and tree shadows flickered on her face. And it would have been easy to stay with her, thought Ky, preferable too. But he did not belong to Merion. He was a student from the Academy, from the Federation of Planets, and sooner or later he would have to return there. And the longer he stayed with Celise, the harder the leaving would be.

'It's best if I go,' he said firmly.

'I'll wait,' Celise offered.

'What's the point?'

'I'll wait anyway. You might change your mind.'

There was nothing Ky could say. She did as she chose to do and he was aware of her dark eyes watching as he walked away, and a pang of regret. It was as if he were turning his back on something beautiful and vital and barely understood . . . not just Celise, but Merion itself, a people, a culture, a little pocket of peace and stability in an unstable universe. It was like crossing a line between life and death. Ahead of him was Hal-Arrison's ship, the strife of worlds and civilizations and his own future, a line of dark diggings and two men who did not like each other very much. The heat was brittle, the silence menacing, and the death flower waited with her briars and thorns, her seed heavy in his pocket. Dry grass snapped beneath his shoes as he approached.

'Here's our student!' Dr Largo exclaimed.

Ky put down his bag.

'You want some help?'

'Of course, of course,' the little man said genially.

Hal-Arrison leaned on his spade.

'I thought I told you to stay in the village!'

'It's opting out,' said Ky.

'Of what?' Hal-Arrison asked him.

Not really knowing, Ky shrugged his shoulders. It was not too late. Celise was waiting and he could go back there. Or maybe he had a part to play in the scheme of things? Undecided, he stood on the edge of the trench, watched for a moment as Dr Largo sifted soil through a sieve. The seeds were winged like insects but he did not see one, and all the specimen jars remained empty.

'How long will you search?' he asked.

'Until we find,' Hal-Arrison retorted.

'What if you don't?'

'Then we'll leave, won't we?'

'So how long will you search?'

'For crying out loud!'

Dr Largo put down the sieve.

His pale eyes gleamed with excitement.

And he was looking at Ky.

'I think we need search no further,' he said. 'Such a timely arrival has to be propitious. I had begun to fear I would have to return to the Galactic Council and confess I'd failed in my mission. But now you're here . . .'

He pulled out his revolver.

And turned to Hal-Arrison.

'I want no interference,' Dr Largo said.

'What the hell are you doing?'

'Inside the ship, if you please.'

'Put that damned thing away!'

Sunlight shining on Dr Largo's spectacles made him eyeless, and he was only a little man, but as Hal-Arrison lunged towards him he pulled the trigger. He was shot in the leg, thought Ky, or maybe not. He just saw him collapse in a moment of shock and horror, as Celise screamed among the distant trees and Dr Largo turned the gun on him. Only a little man . . . but his expression was ruthless and his voice was menacing and fear lurched in Ky's stomach. Ben Utha forbade, Dr Largo said, and he had agreed to harm nothing on Merion, but that could hardly apply to Ky. He was a student from the Academy, from the Federation of Planets, and one student was no great loss.

'A small price to pay for the salvation of a planet,' said Dr Largo. 'Don't you agree?'

'You're mad!' said Ky.

The little man smiled.

'It's not personal, of course. Just a short walk among the brambles . . .'

Ky picked up his travel bag, aimed a swipe as Celise came running across the sand and Hal-Arrison cried out a warning. It was all ineffectual. Dr Largo seemed to possess a manic strength, a single-mindedness that could not be distracted. One podgy arm warded off the blows and the bag was wrenched from Ky's hand. Hard fingers gripped his wrist, twisted and thrust and propelled him forward, headlong into the arms of the death flower.

Then there was nothing but his own terror and the thorns raking him, tangling in his clothes and his hair. Pale eyes watched as he screamed and struggled, and smilingly Dr Largo held Celise at bay. Black and scarlet, the colours flashed on the edges of Ky's vision, and the seeds swarmed upwards, fed on his fear and blood.

*

Afterwards Ky did not remember very much . . . just a chaos of people, hands and faces, voices and colours. Scratches bled and throbbed and merged into a single agony and his mind drifted in and out of consciousness. They must have carried him to the village. He saw dark mist rising from the lake, sunset through a window, heard Hal-Arrison talking. Then someone made him drink from a cupful of bitter liquid and the darkness grew complete for a while.

When he awoke he was lying on a bed in a midnight room where a small lamp flickered. His throat felt parched, his whole body dry and hot and burning, pulsing with pain. An old woman, moving among shadows, sponged his body, made him drink of the same bitter brew until he slept again.

Then the dreams began. There were seeds in his flesh that germinated and put down roots. He could feel them in the channels of his arteries and veins, working their way towards his heart. Small shoots sprouted from his fingertips and there were leaves and thorns in his hair. He was being devoured. And he thrashed against the terror of extinction, against the loss of his own identity, and the girl that called a name he did not know. Her hair was black and her clothes were scarlet and her dark eyes pierced him, sharp as thorns. He lashed out at her and she went away but the death flower remained inside him.

There was no one to help him, no one to soothe him, only Hal-Arrison with his blond hair and violet eyes sitting beside his bed. Somehow Ky still knew him, but he seemed to fade pale-faced into distances and his own pain, gave way to others whom he did not know and could not understand. Voices hushed him, hands held him, but they could not reach him. They belonged to another world where darkness and light changed places and he was not. He only existed inside himself, a nameless someone sinking deeper and deeper into a

103

body whose wounds festered and suppurated, or else healed into agonizing lines of tightness, where he dreamed and screamed and was unable to escape from the death flower sharing his skin.

It was a kind of battle and slowly Ky gave up the fight, grew weaker as she grew stronger. His breathing turned shallow, his heartbeats faltered and faded, and his flesh turned to fibre as her pale roots crept. She was feeding on the life of him, squeezing him out, and the space of his body was not enough for both of them. He left as her flowers bloomed in his mind . . . and he found himself alive. It was a strange experience. Suddenly Ky was outside himself, floating near the ceiling and looking down at a body on the bed that had once been his. It was not any more, although a shining silvery thread still connected him to it. It was dead, he thought. Yet he was alive; his seeing, his hearing, his perception more acute than it had ever been before, as if reality were enhanced. He could see beyond the window the brilliance of the daylight, and the radiance of colours woven in the mat on the floor, the depth in the shine on the polished brass lamp. He could see every strand of the old woman's hair and the blue knotted veins on her hand, and in the lines of Ben Utha's face every mark and emotion of his life. He smelled ointment and incense and flowers in the courtyard, and he heard what they said to each other.

'He's gone, I think.'

'And he so young,' Ben Utha said sadly.

'We did all we could,' the old woman murmured.

'Hal-Arrison will grieve,' said Ben Utha.

'Celise too,' the old woman said.

'So much loss,' said Ben Utha, 'in a single life.'

Ky wanted to tell them.

He was not dead.

But the door opened and Hal-Arrison, leaning on a crutch, came limping in. His face was haggard, his blond hair uncombed, his left leg heavily bandaged and his navy blue flying suit cut away at the knee. Ashen with pain he dragged himself to the bed.

'Has he made it past the crisis?'

'Just a moment ago,' Ben Utha said.

'I got here as quickly as I could.'

'And you are too late,' Ben Utha said.

'You mean he's dead?'

'When the soul departs the body we are bound to accept . . .'

'No!' Hal-Arrison said harshly. 'I'm not accepting that! He can't do this to me! He was placed in my care and I'm responsible! Ky? Do you hear me? Don't you dare die on me! Not for X33 and a sodding flower! Your life's more important than that!'

He leaned and balanced and shook Ky's shoulder, as if he would shake him awake. And through the slender silvery thread Ky felt his touch, an irresistible connection drawing him back inside his body again. There was a lurch of his heartbeat restarting, the knowledge of his own skin tight as a glove and a thousand superficial hurts. But his life was important, his part in the scheme of things, and individuals always mattered. He opened his eyes. He was lying in bed, gazing up at Hal-Arrison, a man and his emotions, the trace of a tear and a slow laconic smile. His dry lips cracked as he spoke.

'Did he find it?'

'Did who find what?' Hal-Arrison asked.

'Did Dr Largo find the seed of the death flower?'

Ky's body healed and was young, but inside he knew he was immortal, and physical life was, just a temporary thing. He thought of it often in the days that followed, as the old woman tended him as his scratches faded to scars. Things that had mattered to him once mattered nothing at all to him now. Academic achievements, future career, the acquisition of wealth or position or power, all that was acceptable and desirable among the Federation of Planets was no longer important, because he knew when he finally died he could take nothing with him except himself. Ambition was redundant and he was irreversibly changed. He had no choice but to live as they lived on Merion, grow like Ben Utha, an old man with the years shining serenely from his eyes, untouched by all that went on elsewhere.

Yet he did not belong on Merion and he thought he never would. He was isolated by his own experience. Not even Ben Utha remembered the death flower. No one did. It had been dormant since before they were born and they had no direct knowledge of the thing. They had been taught by their parents and grandparents how to live wisely, and now they taught their children. Celise was beautiful because she had been brought up that way. It was an already established lifestyle, a kind of conformity which she never questioned. But Ky had come to it another way, through pain and terror and that strange recognition of what it meant to be alive.

And what had happened to him, what had occurred, was never talked about and never discussed . . . no mention of Dr Largo and what he had done, the rights and wrongs of it and the possible consequences. Ky could only suppose he remained with the ship, tending the seeds of the death flower. But if he asked his questions were ignored or brushed aside, and even Hal-Arrison had no idea. Nor did he care.

'May he rot in hell!' Hal-Arrison said angrily.

And maybe he had cause to be bitter. There were splinters of bone embedded in the flesh of his leg and the wound went deep. He would probably limp for the rest of his life, Celise confided. And now he was grounded, unable to walk without a crutch, and Ky along with him. Healing took time, the old woman said. And where else did they want to be apart from Merion?

Days turned to weeks and the planet acted like a drug, erasing both past and future. It was as if the universe ceased to exist. Quiet people went about their quiet lives and turned their backs on whatever might trouble them, not wanting to know. Almost it was easy to forget. In Ben Utha's house no windows opened on to the fields or overlooked the promontory, the northern skyline where the ship was parked and the jungles of the death flower began. In communal evenings everyone danced and sang. And the days were long, full of work and sun, and time spent sitting in the courtyard where tree shade flickered on the pool and massed flowers bent over their own reflections. Idyllic, thought Ky. But how long could they go on?

'I'd like to stay here forever,' Hal-Arrison murmured.

'And will we?' Ky asked him.

'What could be nicer?' Hal-Arrison said.

Ky frowned.

The idea was tempting. They could build a house by the lake, work in the fields, live out their lives and forget. And if forgetting was impossible then they could choose to ignore the universe and all that went on in it.

'It's not our problem anyway,' said Ky.

'What isn't?' Hal-Arrison inquired.

'X33,' said Ky. 'And the decision made by the Galactic Council. Dr Largo and the death flower. It's not our problem.'

'Not if we stay here,' Hal-Arrison agreed.

'Unless Merion gets attacked,' said Ky.

'An unlikely event,' Hal-Arrison retorted.

'But suppose it does,' said Ky. 'Suppose X33 invents the hyper-drive unit and begins to colonize. Merion's defenceless . . . so what would happen?'

'Presumably the Galactic Council would mobilize the fleet.'

'You mean someone has to take the responsibility?'

'Well, obviously,' Hal-Arrison said.

'But not us?' asked Ky.

Hal-Arrison reached for his crutch.

His face twisted as he rose to his feet.

'Damn you!' he said.

Ky watched him as he limped away, a man with violet

eyes and sunlight on his hair. It seemed he had not wished to be reminded. Yet he was not the kind of man to opt out, not really, not in the end. And right from the beginning he must have known what this trip was about. And however much he deplored it he must have agreed to carry it out . . . not for the hire fees paid for his ship or because he was commandeered, but because he believed it was right. And maybe it *was* right, thought Ky. Maybe it was as necessary to protect worlds from attack and self-destruction as it was to protect individuals. And someone had to take the responsibility . . . the Galactic Council, Hal-Arrison, Dr Largo and Ky.

Later Hal-Arrison returned to find him.

'I think we should leave,' he said.

When?' asked Ky.

'Now,' said Hal-Arrison.

'And you need me to pilot the ship?'

'I doubt if Dr Largo has any idea.'

Ky smiled.

From a flight simulator to the reality . . . it was all part of the training. A mere achievement, he thought, but necessary if he wanted to remain at the Academy and continue to live within the Federation of Planets where achievement counted. And he could not turn his back on the universe as they did on Merion, nor could he choose to ignore it. Because it was there . . . just as surely as the death flower was there . . . its scent on the wind, reborn from his fear and his blood. He went upstairs to pack his travel bag and find Celise.

'I have to go,' he told her.

She stared at him in disbelief.

Then tears filled her eyes.

'But why?' she cried. 'I thought you were happy here. I thought you would stay. What can you possibly want that Merion can't offer?'

'Nothing,' he said.

'Then why must you go?'

He spread his hands.

She had been incurious from the beginning and he could not begin to explain. And her ways were not the ways of the universe so she had no need to understand. And the scent of the death flower was everywhere, bittersweet and pervading. She closed the window with a bang.

'You're surely not going for *that*?' she said.

Ky picked up his bag.

The death flower was a part of him and he could hardly refuse to accept it, no more than they had refused to accept it on Merion once upon a time. It was as real for Ky as it had been for Ben Utha's parents or grandparents, but to Celise it was merely symbolic, like the paper-weight in his pocket, a small shrivelled seed of a thing preserved in glass. And symbols were not enough. They were like legends, or religions, or historical accounts . . . powerless to change people, in spite of their significance. It was not enough to know or be told, as Ky had been told about the death flower. Only the direct experience could reveal the fallacies of life as he had known it and offer him a choice. And only the direct experience could change the course of the civilization on X33. Maybe that planet needed the death flower, just as Merion had once needed it, alive and blooming to save it from itself?

'Is it so terrible?' he asked.

Celise did not answer.

Quietly and deliberately, she turned her back.

And there Ky left her, a girl standing by the open window, staring at the lake and not wanting to know. On Merion they lived wisely and could afford to do that, but on X33 they had yet to learn. And this time no one called him, tugged at his heartstrings or waited to be discovered. His stay on Merion was truly over and, slowly, with Hal-Arrison, he walked through the fields towards the promontory.

It was no longer summer. The grasses were seeding and a few yellowing leaves drifted from the trees. He smelled autumn and evening and the scent of the death flower growing stronger as they approached. She was certainly spectacular. All along the jungle's edge she was ablaze with green and scarlet, glossy leaves and waxen flowers and blue-black seed heads. In places she had advanced almost to the water's edge, her thorny branches embracing the ship and almost smothering it.

Hal-Arrison stopped walking.

Leaning heavily on his crutches he stood and stared.

'It seems our decision has been taken for us,' he said.

'What do you mean?' Ky asked him.

'There's no way through. We'll *have* to stay on Merion.'

'She's only a plant,' said Ky.

'How can you say that? You of all people?'

'Because it's true,' said Ky.

'Aren't you afraid?'

'No,' said Ky.

Hal-Arrison had taught him that once. There was nothing to fear but fear, and that was in himself. It was nothing to do with the death flower. Unconcerned he walked towards her, ducked beneath her branches, using the travel bag to force a way through. Leaves brushed his face, and fallen petals lay like pools of blood, and her thorns raked him. But scratches hardly mattered. She had scratched him before and he knew he would survive. And all around the seed heads burst and the winged seeds scattered and fell.

'Where's Dr Largo?' Hal-Arrison shouted from behind him.

'I don't know,' shouted Ky.

And the ship was empty. Branches grew in through the open hatch, and flowers bloomed among the seats, and the floor was littered with seeds. Nothing remained of Dr Largo . . . only a pair of spectacles, a soiled sun hat and a rack of empty specimen jars waiting to be filled. He must have been afraid, thought Ky. In the end, alone with the death flower, he must have realized he was an individual and been afraid. He squatted down between the seats and scooped up the seeds . . . a present from Merion, the meaning of life, the greatest gift of all. Someone had to do it, he thought. On X33, over Asia, Europe and America, over all the continents someone had to scatter the seeds of the death flower.

And Hal-Arrison watched him.

'We could go straight back to the Academy,' he said.

'Could we?' said Ky.

5

The Silver Box

There was nothing special about number Forty-Seven. It was indistinguishable from all the other houses in Gossington Square, part of a Victorian terrace divided into flats, its stone facade showing signs of decay. Rooms were big and gloomy and full of draughts, and during the day most of the residents were out. Carole took a throat lozenge from the silver box, sat on the window seat and watched the snow. Lime trees at the centre of the Square looked black against the whirling whiteness and the street was empty of traffic and people. Except for Carole the house was empty too . . . everyone away at work . . . her mother teaching at the comprehensive school . . . Mrs Dawkins from downstairs helping in the Oxfam shop . . . and the man from the basement gone to his office. And overhead the attic flat was once more unoccupied. Someone had died there, Mrs Dawkins claimed. A housemaid whose sweetheart had been killed in the First World War had committed suicide, and no one stayed for very long. Carole did not believe in ghosts, but the house creaked with stillness and the silence oppressed her. She was sick of being alone.

She had glandular fever, the doctor said. It was caused by a virus and was slightly contagious so she should not return to school until after Easter. Now it was January and Carole had nothing to look forward to for the next three months but paracetamols and a pain in the neck, headaches and fatigue and feelings of grottiness, and a fluctuating temperature that made reality look strange. Perspectives were unstable. Walls seemed either too near, or too far away. The floor had a slope to it and the wind rattling the window got on her nerves.

Carole shivered and returned to bed. A sensible move, except that most of it was occupied by a fat black and white cat. Officially Splodge belonged to Mrs Dawkins and was there on loan to keep Carole company until Mrs Dawkins returned at one o'clock to prepare the lunch. But all he ever did was sleep, warm and heavy in the place where her legs ought to be. 'Shove over, you great dozy beast!' Carole said irritably. Green eyes opened, glared at her in annoyance, before he curled and settled again in the crook of her knees. When Splodge was sleeping, Mrs Dawkins said, he did not like to be disturbed. And, out of consideration, Carole was trapped there for the rest of the morning.

Lonely and boring, the hours stretched endlessly ahead. She might have switched on the radio or studied her school books, but listening to music made her headache worse and she could not concentrate. Curled with the cat she tried to sleep but then she grew hot and sweaty and small sounds distracted her . . . the whine of the wind down the boarded-up chimney, the flutter of snow against the window pane, and the creak of a floorboard. It was as if someone were there, quietly moving at the far end of her room. Carole raised her head. She saw nothing unusual . . . just a shimmer of heated air above the electric convector heater and the walls receding into distances, the effects of her fever. But the sounds went on, movements and footsteps, soft and disturbing. And did she imagine the room was growing dark?

There was a humming noise too, like high frequency static almost beyond the range of her hearing. Once more Carole raised her head and for one panic-stricken moment she thought she was going blind. There was light around her bed but the rest of the room had

113

vanished, dissolved in a curtain of shimmering air and darkness beyond it. Or maybe something was wrong with the convector heater? The electronic hum was clearer now, increasing in pitch. Even the cat could hear it. And they moved together, Carole and Splodge, propelled by the same fear. He rose from the bed with green eyes blazing, arched and spat and bolted for the door, his tail bushed as a fox's brush . . . and she switched off the convector heater and made to follow.

But the humming noise ceased and the shimmering grew steady, hung as a veil of sheer air from ceiling to floor, and beyond it the room was still there. Carole paused to stare, her curiosity conquering her fear. It was as if she were seeing into another world. It was morning where she stood but there it was night. A full moon shone through a broken window and trees in leaf made flickering shadows on the floor. She could smell warmth and flowers and sweet summer air, and in the room a smell of musty decay. She sensed, rather than saw, that time had changed. The house was old. Paper peeled from the walls, the ceiling sagged and the floorboards rotted. It was long ago, thought Carole, or maybe not. She noticed wires and cables, arc lights and cameras and video-recorder, computer terminals and electronic equipment. It was as if her room had been turned into a television studio or the set for a horror film.

Unless she was dreaming?

'Hold it!' said a voice.

'What now?' asked another.

'There's a definite energy reading here.'

'It's probably a rat.'

'Just let me check.'

Suddenly someone appeared beyond the wall of wavering air. For all it was dark at that end of the room Carole could see him quite clearly . . . a boy in a black cat-suit, his fair curls blowing in the wind. She saw the silver shine of his wristwatch, slim limbs and the flash of his smile. And through him she saw the window frame, the moon through his face, the stars behind his eyes. He was there and yet not there. Beautiful, she thought, and as transparent as a ghost.

'Hey, Zak!' he said excitedly. 'Come and take a look!'

'No way, screwball!' the other replied. 'I'm not falling for that one again.'

'This is for real, Zak. We've actually got one!'

'A grey rat or black?'

'A girl standing by an antique bed. She has long brown hair and is wearing a floral nightdress buttoned to the neck. It's pink and old-fashioned and she's very pale. We've done it, Zak!'

'Bullshit!' Zak replied.

He too came suddenly into view . . . another ghost, big and bearded and bespectacled, scruffy as a student, with some unreadable slogan printed on the whiteness of his T-shirt. By his accent Carole guessed he was American and although he stared directly at her she had the peculiar feeling he was unable to see her, that in some way she was invisible. His words confirmed it.

'You're imagining things, buddy.'

'What do you mean?' the fair one asked.

'There's nothing there but the wall.'

'Don't be ridiculous! She's as clear as day!'

'Are you bullshitting me, Matt?'

'No,' Matt said earnestly. 'I'm telling you, Zak. Believe me . . . she *is* there.'

Carole was there all right. She had long brown hair and was wearing a floral nightdress just as Matt had described. But Zak saw no one and nor was he about to be convinced. The experimenter influenced the experiment, he said, and Matt was seeing what he wanted to see. His own hyped mind had produced the energy reading, *and* Carole. She was a mental projection, not a genuine phenomenon. Matt shifted the tripod and set up the camera. Seeing was believing, he retorted, and he believed Carole was real. And on heat-sensitive film her outline was bound to show. She watched him in annoyance. He did not behave as if she were real. He did not ask permission or ask if she minded, explain who he was or what he was doing there.

'Smile, please,' he told her.

And something snapped.

'Get out of my bedroom!' Carole said. 'You've got no right to come barging in here and take my photograph! Who the hell do you think you are?'

Matt seemed to freeze in the flickering moonlight.

Then clutched Zak's arm.

'Did you hear that?' he said.

'What?' asked Zak.

'She spoke.'

'Leave it out!'

'I'm telling you, Zak. Who the hell are we, she said.'

It was a peculiar meeting . . . Matt in the midnight darkness and Carole in the morning light with the veiled air shimmering between them. His full name was Matthew Boyd-Hamilton with a hyphen, he said, and Zak was over from the United States on a two-year student exchange. They were both studying para-psychology at the nearby university and Carole was vital to their experiment. She did not understand the technicalities of time displacement and psychokinetic trace-ability, but she agreed to take part. After all, Matt was very good-looking even if he was a ghost, and talking to him was better than being bored and alone.

'So what do you want me to do?' she asked him.

'Scientifically,' he said, 'we need to prove you exist.'

'Isn't it obvious?'

'To you and me, maybe. But say-so isn't enough. It's not enough to convince Zak, let alone the board of examiners.'

'So what do you want me to do?' Carole repeated.

Zak, who was an electronics expert, set up the equipment and ran through a series of tests. Portable computers flickered and buzzed but apart from the original bleep of the energy pulse Carole failed to register. Nor did she show on the heat-sensitive video-camera, in infra-red or ultra-violet light. Except to Matt she remained invisible and inaudible, her existence unproven. In other words, said Zak, she was not really there.

'Are you calling me a liar?' asked Matt.

Carole took a throat lozenge from the silver box and waited while they argued. Whatever Carole was, said Matt, a mental projection or an independent entity, they needed to find out. And when high technology failed, human minds came into their own. Zak's machines were not infallible. And what was wrong with a tape-recorder and common sense? If they could verify whatever information Carole gave them . . .

'If,' said Zak.

'It's worth a try,' said Matt.

'Would you like a blackcurrant throat sweet?' asked Carole.

'No,' said Matt . . . then turned towards her, as if he suddenly remembered she was there. 'No, thanks,' he said. 'If you touch the circuit you'll probably break it and we're not into experiments of telekinesis.'

'What's she saying?' Zak asked suspiciously.

'She says . . .'

Matt hesitated, regarded Carole thoughtfully, as if for a moment he too doubted her reality or else she had no right to be chewing sweets in his company. She closed the box, saw his eyes following her movements, the pressure of her fingers on the hinged lid.

'What's wrong?' she asked him.

'Nothing,' he said.

'That's what I mean,' said Zak. 'If everything she says is inaudible it's not going to work, is it?'

But it did work. For the benefit of Zak and the tape-recorder Matt repeated everything Carole said. It was very mundane, just details of her name and age, where and when she had been born, which Zak intended to check with the Central Records Office. And even that much seemed questionable, as if the date of her birth was not as they had expected. She had to produce the calendar for confirmation. She had been born sixteen years ago, she insisted, and now it was 1987 . . . January 21st, 1987. Outside it was snowing . . . Mrs Thatcher was Prime Minister . . . and why on earth should she remember the First World War?

'Zak?' said Matt.

'Yeh,' said Zak. 'I heard.'

'Someone's goofed. Your time displacement machine has got to be faulty.'

'How about your imagination, buddy?'

'If I were making her up she'd fit the preconceived image,' argued Matt. 'She'd have a mop and a feather duster and the date would be 1917. Right? That means . . .'

'Okay!' said Zak. 'That suggests she's genuine, existing in her own right and nothing to do with you. But *if* she's genuine, how come I don't see her? And how come on all this psycho-sensitive equipment she doesn't show?'

Matt shook his head. The moon was gone and infrared light made all things colourless, stripped him of clarity and dissolved him to a shadow, as if he were hardly there at all. And Zak too was no more than a grey shade restlessly prowling, checking and re-checking the vision screens and print-outs, leaving his footprints on the dusty floor. He made Carole feel responsible, as if she ought to apologize for being what she was. Instead she shivered, not knowing what to say.

The room had grown cold without the convector heater. She could feel the chill of the night wind through the broken window and Matt's eyes watching her, intense and curious, as she reached for her dressing gown. It was pale blue quilted, she heard him tell Zak, and she was obviously sensitive to temperature, reacting to her own space-time environment. And now she was

taking a blackcurrant throat lozenge from a silver box . . .
similar to a box his mother had at home on her dressing
table which had been handed down through the family.

'You want me to go on?' asked Matt.

'No,' growled Zak. 'I've heard enough!'

'It's odd, don't you think?'

'You ought to be on stage, Boyd-Hamilton!'

'Two blackcurrant lozenges in half an hour . . . why
should I imagine that?'

'I've got glandular fever,' Carole told him.

'She says she has glandular fever,' said Matt.

'What?' Zak said sharply.

'Glandular fever,' Matt repeated.

There was a moment of silence.

'Shucks!' said Zak. 'I take it all back.'

'You mean I've finally said something right?' asked
Carole.

Matt smiled, picked up a fragment of mortar from the
floor and aimlessly threw it. It should have landed at
Carole's feet but the shimmering air absorbed it,
absorbed the throat lozenge Carole aimed at him. He
smiled again at her effort. It was a barrier, he said, which
nothing could pass through and it was not just space
between them but time as well. He glanced at his
wristwatch. One hundred and thirty five years, six
months, two days and fourteen hours to be precise, he
said. In his time it was July 23rd, 2121.

Carole gaped at him. Even when Matt explained it was
not imaginable. She could not envisage a hundred and
thirty-five years into the future. England was ruled from
Brussels, he told her. Energy came from the sun and
there was no nuclear war, no major world problems and
not much political dissension. The holes in the ozone
layer were healing and the latest American space ship
was about to take off for the stars. There was not a soul
left alive who remembered when Carole lived. The
twentieth century was ancient history and Gossington
Square was derelict and due to be demolished.

'That's why we're here,' said Matt. 'There aren't many old houses left. This is the only one in the area which is empty and reputed to be haunted. It's not exactly safe but we had to take the chance. A couple of weeks from now the house will be flattened and its ghosts will be gone.'

'Are you saying you're a ghost-buster?' Carole asked him.

'That's right,' said Matt. 'And you're busted. We were hoping for the housemaid who committed suicide but we'll settle for you.'

'I'm not a ghost!' Carole said indignantly.

'Aren't you?' Matt said quietly.

Her insides lurched. His smile was sad and he was looking at her gently, tenderly, not wanting to distress her but wanting her to understand . . . from where he stood, one hundred and thirty-five years in the future, Carole was dead. She thought she must have died without knowing it, that very morning, before she had even lived. She wanted to scream and deny it, tell him he was wrong, that she was still alive and would go on living, but then Mrs Dawkins came into the room.

'How are you feeling, my dear?'

Carole froze, looked towards Matt, but it seemed Mrs Dawkins did not see him. She simply walked through the curtain of shimmering air and picked up the throat lozenge that lay on the carpet . . . and as she did so, everything vanished. The room was as it had been before, wintry and cold, with snow fluttering against the window pane and the clock on the mantelpiece saying ten past one.

Carole was dead, Matt had said, but she did not tell her mother. Even to her own mind it seemed crazy. Yet she needed to convince herself she was alive. She noticed the heat in the bathroom and the scent of talc, the taste of kedgeree her mother cooked for supper. And that night she lay awake feeling the blankets rough and warm to her touch, remembering the television serial she had sat and watched, hearing the tick of the clock, the rattle of the window and the whine of the wind in the chimney breast. All those things assured her she was alive. Unless they were illusions. Maybe, she thought, life was a dream and when she awoke she would find herself dead? Or maybe Matt had been an omen? A cold moon shone on the snow in Gossington Square and she was afraid to sleep, afraid to let go of her awareness of herself and the world. And in the morning, when her mother drew back the curtains, Carole was pale and tired and dark shadows ringed her eyes. She looked like death warmed up, her mother said.

'Maybe it's terminal,' Carole said agitatedly.

'What?' inquired her mother.

'Glandular fever.'

'That's highly unlikely,' her mother replied.

It was a kind of reassurance and Carole's own common sense told her that ghosts didn't need to eat breakfast or write school essays, did not stub their toes on the table leg or suffer from headaches and swollen glands. They did not fancy other ghosts either, but Carole spent the morning waiting and hoping Matt would return, materialize from the thin air of her room . . . a ghost from the future as she was a ghost from the past. Nothing happened. Her eyes grew leaden and heat shimmered above the convector fire . . . and Mrs Dawkins woke her at one o'clock with chicken soup for lunch.

Had it not been for Splodge, Carole might have believed she had invented the whole incident. But that cat was behaving very peculiarly, Mrs Dawkins said. He had spent yesterday afternoon and evening crouching behind the sofa and refusing to come out. And earlier that morning, when Mrs Dawkins had picked him up intending to bring him upstairs for Carole, he had sworn and struggled like a wildcat and finally scratched her, fled downstairs to the basement boiler room and escaped through the partly open window.

'I can't think what's come over him,' Mrs Dawkins said worriedly.

Carole knew. A couple of ghost-busters from AD 2121 had scared Splodge half to death. And all afternoon she heard Mrs Dawkins calling across the back gardens. It made her feel guilty thinking of Splodge out in the cold snow, cowering among the cabbages and afraid to come home, while she sat by the convector heater wanting nothing more than for Matt and Zak to reappear and feeling disappointed they did not.

Cats had short memories. Splodge returned the following morning, but as the days went by Carole's disappointment turned to depression. The snow melted and snowdrops bloomed beneath the lime trees in the Square and Matt's absence haunted her. She thought she would not have minded if he *had* proved her to be a ghost because her life, as it was, was hardly worth living. She was sick of having glandular fever, sick of being confined to the house, fed up with everything.

'I might as well be dead!' she announced.

Her mother was marking school exercise books.

'Why's that?' she said.

'Well, what's there to live for?' Carole asked.

'There's next week's episode of "Dallas".'

'Who cares about "Dallas"?'

'Tomorrow's dinner then?'

'I'm being serious,' Carole said cuttingly.

'So am I,' her mother replied. 'What else do we live for but the little mundane things of life? If we sit around waiting for the few rare, wonderful moments that make it all worthwhile we may as well not live at all.'

'That's what I meant!' said Carole.

'You'll get over it,' her mother promised.

Splodge got over it. Accompanied by Mrs Dawkins he made a few nervous forays into Carole's room and, finding nothing to alarm him, took up residency again on the candlewick counterpane. He was better than no one, Carole supposed. And when February began with two days of freezing rain she followed Splodge's example, sighed and forgot . . . until she woke that night and saw beyond the wall of shimmering air the room full of sunset light and Matt standing there. It was four in the morning according to the clock on the mantelpiece and Carole did not know if she were glad or furious, or how to react.

'Where have you been?' she hissed.

'Checking,' he told her.

'Where's Zak?'

'He's checking too . . . the Central Records Office.'

Carole draped her dressing gown around her shoulders.

'So how long does it take?' she asked him. 'You've been checking for ten days already and all I gave you was my name and address!'

Matt looked surprised. The sunset was brassy behind him and trees drooped in the summer heat. Owls hooted in the derelict Square. When Mrs Dawkins had entered the room the time circuit had snapped, he explained. He had tried to get back to her as quickly as possible but obviously the passage of time in past and future was not the same. Carole's ten days was his yesterday and his early evening was the middle of her night.

'I'm sorry,' he said honestly.

She was glad anyway, glad he was back, but with her mother sleeping in the next bedroom their conversation had to be in whispers. He needed to talk to her, he said, alone, before Zak returned from the Central Records Office. Something had been worrying him, nagging at his mind ever since Carole had first appeared. It was not just the fact that he could see and hear her and Zak could not, nor was it the fact that the machines failed to register her presence . . . it was the fact that her behaviour was inconsistent with any known psychic phenomenon. In other words she did not act like a ghost.

'Nor do you,' Carole told him.

'Well, I'm not a ghost,' he said.

'Yes, you are,' said Carole. 'You don't have any

123

substance and I can see straight through you, so what else can you be? And if I'm dead to you then you're dead to me . . . or rather, you're not yet born. I mean, why should I have to prove I'm real when you're not real either?'

Matt stared at her.

'I don't understand,' he said.

'Now you know how I feel,' Carole told him.

Matt ran a hand through his blond unruly curls. He was as confused as she had been for the last ten days, her mind going round and round in circles trying to work it out. Now it was his turn to think himself a ghost. She could see the stones of the wall through the cat-suit he was wearing, the broken window through his eyes. They were blue, she thought, bright as a midday sky. But the impression faded among leaves of trees and the roseate hues of sunset. She was a ghost seeing a ghost and was tempted to laugh, but maybe it was not so funny. Surrounded by midwinter darkness and all the trappings of her own reality, Carole ached with the sheer impossibility of knowing him.

'What *is* this?' he asked her.

'I don't know,' she replied.

'I'm alive, so I can't be a ghost.'

'In that case I'm not one either because I'm alive too.'

'That's impossible.'

'But it's true,' said Carole.

'Zak's never going to believe it.'

'But you do?' Carole asked anxiously.

'I suppose that's why I wanted to talk to you,' he said.

'So what do we do now?'

'Prove it?' he sighed.

Carole approached the veil of shimmering air. Matt was beyond it, so close that she thought she could touch him if she reached out her hand. Maybe he read her mind and knew her feelings, wanted her to be real just as she wanted him. Or maybe they did not think at all. Time had no meaning until Carole stepped into it and found

124

herself alone. The room was dark. Rain lashed the window glass. Matt and the summer world and the hoot of owls were gone.

Several days passed before Matt reappeared. Carole was sitting in the armchair beside the convector heater writing an essay on the French Revolution, when she heard the hum of the time displacement machine. She held her breath as the shimmering air dissolved the walls and window and the morning faded to a future midnight. Both Matt and Zak were there but she had no chance to speak to them for Splodge, asleep on the bed, suddenly awoke and was aware. He seemed to go berserk, a mad cat spitting and swearing and trying to escape. Ears flattened, tail fluffed, and belly touching the floor, he headed for the door, found it shut and fled beneath the bed, emerged on the other side and shot through the time barrier before Carole could stop him. Claws raked the velvet curtains. Jigsaws and the Monopoly set, stored on top of the wardrobe, fell as he leapt. And there he stayed, cowering behind a wicker basket full of dolls' clothes, peering down with green eyes bigger than gobstoppers and a slightly puzzled expression on his splodgy black and white face. He had broken the circuit. The room was as it should be. February sunlight lay bright on the pink patterned carpet and only Carole was mad.

'You great stupid idiot!' she yelled.

She left the door open, spent the rest of the day sorting out thousands of jigsaw pieces, and what should have been a beautiful encounter had been ended before it began. Then her fever, which had abated, returned worse than ever. Her head throbbed, and paracetamols ceased to have any effect, and even in bed she had to wear a wollen scarf tied tight around her neck to ease the pain. Her mother filled hot-water bottles before she left for school and each morning, on her way to the Oxfam shop, Mrs Dawkins looked in and made her a honey and lemon drink. Freezing mist hung outside the window, made ghostly the lime trees that grew in the Square and isolated Carole from the world. Not that she cared. Snuggled in bed with the cat she felt miserable enough to want to be left alone and she was not particularly pleased when the room started buzzing and shimmering. Splodge had another nervous breakdown in his hurry to escape, and Matt and Zak re-established their connections.

'Carole?' said Matt.

Clouds hid the moon and a flashlight shone on crumbling walls, touched the bright elusive blue of his eyes. DON'T BUG ME, the slogan on Zak's T-shirt said. Their voices seemed to come from far away, from a future England in the grip of a heatwave. And how could it be only an hour since Splodge broke the circuit? Only yesterday that Carole had last talked with Matt? Days and weeks were muddled in her head but it was some consolation to learn that she was not about to die of glandular fever. Zak had traced her birth certificate, Matt informed her, but had found no record of her death. Presumably she was going to live and marry and change her name, but as twentieth-century records were not computerized he could not tell her who her future husband would be. Having met Matt, Carole was not really interested anyway, and nor was Zak. Her future was beside the point, he said. And finding her birth certificate might prove she had existed once but it did not prove she existed now, either as a living person or a ghost.

'If she's real we need evidence!' said Zak.

'We could try some awareness tests,' suggested Matt.

'Right now I don't feel like it,' said Carole.

'Yes,' said Matt. 'Something like that. "You feel, therefore you are", and that makes two of us. But I'm not sure about Zak.'

Now and then, Carole could never tell when, but throughout their hot July nights where buff moths fluttered and her February mornings of frost and sun and rain, she tried to convince Zak she was a thinking, feeling, living human being. Her breath made mist on the cold surface of a mirror. She bled when she was scratched, burned when she touched a naked flame. She could deduce, debate, argue, agree or disagree, laugh, cry, hate, love. Yet she could prove nothing because Matt was her only witness and he could be making her up. Not even when she read a passage from a daily paper which checked out verbatim, was Zak convinced. It could be some weird telepathic link-up, he said, Matt's mind picking up vibes from the past.

'What does it take?' Carole asked despairingly.

'About five hundred repeat performances and he might be swayed.' said Matt. 'You know what they say about scientists? If they can't dissect something or examine it under a microscope then it doesn't exist. At least you have God for company.'

'And you,' Carole said softly.

'I'm beginning to wish,' he replied.

'If we were really ghosts . . .'

'Don't,' he said gently.

'If there were just some way . . .'

'There isn't.'

But maybe there was, Carole thought afterwards. Flies caught in amber survived through geological aeons and time capsules were sent into space, or buried under concrete for future generations to find. There had to be something Carole could give that would survive a mere one hundred and thirty-five years, something that would reach Matt and prove to Zak she were real. All night Carole thought of it, eager for morning and needing to act. And it was nothing to do with glandular fever that her eyes shone and her cheeks were flushed. She actually felt better, she told her mother.

Later, when the house was empty and Mrs Dawkins had gone with the shopping trolley to collect the weekly groceries, Carole wrote Matt a letter. She enclosed it with a photograph, a lock of her hair and a blackcurrant throat lozenge, inside the silver box. At home he had one like it, he had said, but this box was Carole's. It was engraved with vine leaves and cherubs and had been given to her by her grandmother before she died. Carefully Carole wrapped it in newspaper and sealed it in a polythene bag. Then she fetched tools from the kitchen, prized away the boarding and placed the package on a ledge in the chimney. Her hands were black with soot and she had to hammer the bent nails straight before she could fix the board back into position. Exertion made her feel ill again but she knew it would be worth it, worth everything to prove herself alive.

February gave way to March. Crocuses bloomed, yellow and purple beneath the lime trees in the Square, and sparrows nested. If the weather was fine, the doctor said, it might do Carole some good to go outside for a breath of fresh air. But she staged a relapse, fearing Matt might appear when she were gone. And the next morning her relapse was genuine. Her head ached, her temperature was up, and the glands in her neck pained something awful. And, spooked once too often, Splodge refused to keep her company, clawed his way from Mrs Dawkins' arms and fled. She spent the day in bed and alone, wondering all over again if she would ever recover.

'Of course you will,' her mother said positively.

'Maybe I don't want to,' Carole said dramatically. 'Maybe I'd rather die and fall in love with a ghost.'

Her mother laughed.

'Love is a symptom of life,' she said. 'But the dead are dead and don't have feelings.'

And that was proof, thought Carole. When Matt read her letter he would know for sure she was alive. Each new day dawned with a kind of nervous anticipation, an experience of relief when her mother went to school and Mrs Dawkins left for the Oxfam shop, a morning of waiting and hoping, another disappointment. Then someone moved into the upstairs flat. A music student with long hair, Mrs Dawkins said disapprovingly. And Carole had something else to contend with. She listened to his footsteps walking the floors overhead, the sound of his radio, the flush of water and the slam of his door. She heard him practising endless scales on a clarinet. He was not intrusive exactly, not over-loud and inconsiderate, yet he was there and she was constantly aware of him. She felt inhibited and no longer free, afraid that when Matt came back she might be overheard and her secret discovered. She wanted the house to herself again, hoped the ghost of the housemaid would drive him away but, to the plaintive notes of a clarinet concerto, it finally happened.

The still air shimmered and wet grey daylight beyond the window slowly darkened to a July night. Carole forgot about the student. There was a thrill inside her and her heart beat faster, and the music was gone in a rumble of thunder and a deluge of summer rain. White with plaster dust and opaque as milk, it dripped through the ceiling and splattered on to the floor, and behind Matt's eyes she saw the lightning flicker, saw the flash of his smile.

'How are you, Carole?'

'Better,' she breathed.

But Zak was in no mood for preliminaries. He was worried about the effects of the lightning on his time displacement machine, about safety factors and the roof falling in and the fact that he was getting wet. Tape-recorder at the ready, Zak simply wanted to collect the routine data and return to the campus. Never mind how Carole was feeling, he said. All Matt needed to ask was the time and date, what the weather was doing and the main newspaper headlines which they could check with the Met. office and archives in the morning . . . then they could both go home.

'Because I'm not hanging around here all night while you chat up the wall,' Zak concluded.

'No one asked you to,' Matt informed him.

'So why don't you stick to the business in hand?'

'Why don't you push off right now?' Matt suggested.

'And leave you in charge of my equipment?' said Zak. 'No way, buddy! Besides, I might miss something.'

Matt sighed, turned to Carole.

'That's the trouble with gooseberries,' he said. 'They're too thick-skinned to understand.'

Carole laughed.

'He will in a minute,' she promised.

'I doubt it,' said Matt.

But Carole had written Matt a letter. It would prove she was real, she said, that she had been aware of him and Zak from the moment she had met them. She had written it down, everything that had happened, all her perceptions and all her feelings. She had put it on a ledge up the chimney, in the silver box. And maybe it was not exactly scientific but it was the only thing she could think of which was part of herself, the only thing she could give Matt which was likely to survive . . . a letter, a lock of her hair and a blackcurrant throat lozenge.

'What's she say?' Zak asked impatiently.

'She says . . .'

Matt shook his head, grinned, then laughed in delight. His eyes shone blue in the torchlight. 'You're beautiful,' he told Carole, and turned away.

'So what's she say?' Zak repeated.

'Wait and I'll show you,' said Matt.

Lightning flashed on the fairness of his hair, and the ceiling dripped and bulged as he approached the chimney breast. There the darkness absorbed him. Carole heard the rotting wood give way as he tore at the boarding, heard Zak's warning cry. She hardly knew what happened next. There was a noise like thunder and her scream mixed with Zak's as the roof beam fell and Matt was buried under tons of rubble. Then there was only Zak, tearing at the stones and plaster chunks and trying to free him, a ghost in the torchlight unashamedly weeping, knowing, when he found him, Matt would be injured or dead.

Carole wept too, loudly and hysterically, not caring that the door opened or who came into the room. He wore blue denim jeans and all she could do was scream at him . . . 'Help him! Help him!' . . . watch as he walked towards the shimmering curtain of air and Zak dragged out the body. 'Dead!' sobbed Zak. 'Oh no . . . not you, Matt!' Then it was over, ended, everything gone. The circuit was broken and Carole was left in the wet grey morning, heart-broken and wretched, with a total stranger.

He spread his hands.

'There was nothing I could do,' he said sadly.

'No,' choked Carole.

'And you don't need to be upset. They were only ghosts and that's how ghosts behave. They relive the moments of their deaths over and over. I've got one upstairs. She walks around my bedroom with a carving knife and there's nothing I can do for her either.'

'You don't understand,' sobbed Carole.

'No one can change the past,' he said gently.

'But Matt lived in the future!' wept Carole. 'And it's my fault he's dead. I didn't need to prove I was real because he knew anyway. If I hadn't put that box up the chimney . . .'

The student was kind and quiet, lending her his handkerchief, making her sit in the kitchen and making her coffee, listening as she talked. He did not say she was crazy or imagining things, or that he himself would have to be mad to believe her. He did not say anything, just listened and waited until she was done. Rain in the ensuing silence fell softly on the roof of the outhouse and the window steamed as Carole wiped her eyes for the thousandth time and finally looked at him. He was staring thoughtfully at the dregs in his coffee cup . . . a young man with fair shoulder-length hair and bright blue eyes. For some reason he reminded her of Matt and once more the silly tears began to flow.

131

'What'll I do?' she whimpered. 'How can I live with it, knowing that I caused his death? How can I bear it?'

He pushed back his chair.

'Maybe you won't have to,' he said. 'It hasn't happened yet, has it? Not for Matt. For him it won't happen for another hundred and thirty-five years. We can't change the past but we can change the future. Do you have a screwdriver or something?'

Uncomprehendingly Carole dragged her mother's tool box from the broom cupboard, watched him select a claw hammer and disappear into the bedroom. The nails gave way easily and he prized away the board that sealed the chimney, returned a minute later with the silver box in his hand. If Carole got rid of it, he said, then Matt would have no reason to go to the chimney breast, no reason to be standing there when the ceiling fell. He would not die and she would not be responsible. And was it really as simple as that?

She watched him open the pedal bin.

'Yes?' he asked.

Carole hesitated. The box was an heirloom. It was old and valuable and somehow it seemed wrong to throw it away. Yet she did not want to keep it. It bound her to Matt and her own memories, to the distant future when he would be living and she would be dead. She supposed she could sell it to an antique shop, but that seemed wrong too.

'Yes?' the student repeated.

'No,' said Carole.

She took it from him, tipped the contents in the bin, then handed it back.

'You keep it,' she said.

He frowned.

'Are you sure?'

'Please,' she said earnestly. 'I'd like you to have it.'

He smiled then, and his smile was like Matt's. He would treasure it, he promised, use it as a paper weight and think of her. Dull silver shone in his hand and she felt it belonged with him, that by giving it to him she had not parted with it at all, or parted with Matt. She had the peculiar feeling that nothing had changed because nothing had happened and the future began in his eyes. She was glad she had met him, grateful for all he had done, for his blond hair and his bright blue eyes and the squeeze of her arm when he turned to go. But Splodge, washing his backside on the landing carpet, took one look at him and fled.

'What's up with the cat?' he asked.

'He thinks he's seen a ghost,' said Carole.

And in a way Splodge had.

'My name, by the way, is John Boyd-Hamilton with a hyphen,' the student said. 'Fancy coming for a pizza on Saturday night?'

6

Mackenna's Patch

The streets were quiet, a thin drizzle falling and a chill wind blowing from the harbour with the noise of ships. Lamplight shone on wet pavements. A loose shutter rattled and a pack of lean dogs fed from the dustbins in the alley. Mackenna had done the rounds, checked the shops—pawn shop and bookmaker, cobbler and corner store and secondhand Rosie's—everywhere locked and barred. He had checked the warehouses by the docks, the derelict factories, the basement workshops on Quay Street. Nothing untoward or out of place . . . only a girl working late in a dingy dressmaker's, long hours for low wages among bales of cloth, tailors' dummies and sewing machines. Mackenna noted her . . . a pretty girl, her fair hair shining under a naked light bulb, intent on her stitching. There was no one else about. The curfew imposed after the rioting twelve months ago still held good. People remained in their homes and Mackenna's patch would stay peaceful until morning.

He yawned and relaxed and poured himself a coffee. Vision screens flickered around him. He could see downhill to the harbour, and uphill to the wasteland where the precinct ended . . . acres of darkness and a high corrugated fence surrounding it. Hoardings advertized soap and chocolate, displayed the anti-government slogans of graffiti writers. And through a dark gap one lone dog disappeared. Nothing remained but the patter of rain, the wet flutter of a newspaper in the gutter and the wind whining around corners.

It was a dreary place to stop. The whole area was dreary . . . decaying buildings full of festering people, a community rife with crime. Not that Mackenna was there himself. He was miles away and warm in the Police Headquarters, but he knew it intimately . . . every crumbling tenement, backstreet drinking house and gambling den . . . every drunk and drop-out, petty thief and prostitute and potential troublemaker. And indirectly they knew him.

He was State Police, licensed to kill. Killing was part of his job. He was quite dispassionate about it and usually a death was deserved. They were lawless people mostly . . . workless, shiftless malcontents . . . human scum whose only contribution to society was an ugliness bred of their own being. Mackenna had no opinions. He simply saw the area reflected in the people . . . foul-mouthed women and dirty children, rough idle men who did little else but drink and brawl. They lived, and died, in a squalor of their own making and blamed, instead, the State or the Welfare Services, the monied upper classes or the unemployment figures. And the rats moved among them, through slums and alleyways and stinking streets, feeding them ideas of a richer, sweeter way of life, stirring them to revolution. It was the rats Mackenna wanted . . . unknown men with unknown faces who talked the truth away.

He yawned again. He might have slept in the warm sound-proofed booth. Many of his comrades did . . . dozed away their duty hours, bored by the inactivity, the long hours of watching while nothing happened. On the East Side and West Side of the city, among the plush houses, maybe they had no reason to stay awake. But Mackenna remained alert, not trusting the quietness, not knowing what the darkness hid. He watched through the camera-lens eyes of the robo-cop, listened through its sensitive antennae, and missed nothing. He saw out

135

at sea the small moving lights of the trawlers. Nearer, he heard the snarl of a dog and a rattle of stones on the wasteland.

Dog meets dog, Mackenna thought.

Or was it a rat?

He leaned forward, suddenly intent, reached for the controls. And the robo-cop obeyed, spun in the air, veered leftwards and rose above the hoardings. The view was clear across dark open spaces, across mounds of stone and rubble, tangled briars and ancient tarmac. He could see the dog, a moving scrap of paleness in the surrounding night. Then, darker than darkness, a shape detached itself from the land and became a person, picked something up to defend itself. The dog backed away as Mackenna homed in, switched on the spotlight and the voice transmitter.

'Stay right where you are!' he said softly.

The boy froze, squinted into the brightness of the light and dropped the stick. Mackenna saw dark hair soaked by rain, saw grey intelligent eyes. He was wearing blue jeans, a navy anorak and new leather trainers and was not from Mackenna's patch. He had been walking some while and was too clean, too well clad.

'Your name and number?' Mackenna inquired.

'Rick Mayo . . . 26/57/361,' the boy replied.

Mackenna fed the number into the computer and waited for confirmation . . . an identity photograph on a vision screen with brief details of a life. He was indeed Rick Mayo, aged seventeen, from 23, Fairgrove Avenue, West Side 5. His parents were Philip John Mayo, a manager of the Federal Banking Corporation, and Ella Mayo née Hadley, a teacher. He had been educated at the West Side High School, gained nine grade-one passes, and was awaiting a place at university. He was a member of the Pole-Cats hardball team, and a member of the city junior athletics team with a sprint speed of . . .

Mackenna did not bother to read on.

'What the hell are *you* doing here?' he said.

Rick spread his hands.

'Just walking.'

'Don't give me that!'

'I had a row with my father and needed to cool off.'

'You know there's a curfew?' Mackenna inquired.

'I never thought.'

'So you don't have a pass?'

'No,' said Rick.

'You're in trouble, sonny.'

'Okay,' said Rick.

'What does that mean?'

Rick shrugged.

'It means okay, I'm in trouble. I guess I'll receive a summons to appear at Police Headquarters for further questioning, along with my father who will no doubt vouch for me . . . in about three months' time, probably. Meanwhile, do I wait here or can I go? Unless you care to arrest me, of course?'

Through the eyes of the robo-cop Mackenna stared at him, memorizing his features, his face. He was used to fear or defiance, downright rudeness or loud-mouthed aggression, but Rick's attitude was glib, almost challenging. Mackenna wondered why. A clever boy who told the truth to hide a lie, perhaps? He knew Mackenna could not hold him, knew it was pointless to prosecute for curfew breaking without some evidence of criminal intent. Rick had intent all right, Mackenna could sense it, although he could not be sure if it were criminal. Yet why else was he there? More than just a walk in the rain after a row with his father, Mackenna thought.

'Can I go?' Rick repeated.

'Beat it!' Mackenna said harshly.

And did he imagine a flicker of surprise in the boy's grey eyes? A touch of relief on his face? Watching him walk away across the wasteland Mackenna felt in his bones that Rick would return, so he stationed the robo-cop in the shadows of a doorway down the street and waited.

Rick wanted to run but he made himself walk, un-hurriedly, back across the wasteland the way he had come, picking a path along old roads between mounds of stones and brambles. He did not know if the robo-cop followed, nor did he dare to look. With hands thrust in pockets he pretended nonchalance, exited through a loose section of fence and let it close behind him with a soft rattle of sound. He was out on the street again, exposed under lamplight, on the edge of West Side where the better quality housing estates began. Thin rain soaked him. He could feel the dampness against his back and was tempted to return home. But instead he waited . . . five minutes, ten . . . checking the time on his wristwatch. Finally, feeling it safe, he turned once again and re-entered the wasteland.

Inside the fence Rick stood motionless, scanning the distances ahead of sky and land for signs of movement. He saw neither the dog nor the robo-cop, although it was too dark to be sure. He advanced warily, kept his footsteps quiet on tussocks of grass, a half brick gripped in his hand ready to lob at glass eye or flesh, whichever confronted him. Small sounds unnerved him . . . the whine of the wind, rain and rustle of leaves, the over-loud thudding of his own heart. Then, at last, he was safely across, searching for the gap between the advertizing hoardings and stepping cautiously into a different street.

Here the rain was in his face, driving inland from the sea with a stench of oil and weed and the fish processing factory. He could see downhill to the harbour, an empty street of sleezy shops and crumbling tenements, and streetlights shining on wet pavements. Somewhere, on the opposite side between the pools of lamplight, was the entrance to an alley. Crouching low Rick made his run, entered the concealing darkness and kept running. Smells rose from dustbins and his soft steps echoed between blank walls of unknown buildings. Memorized instructions flittered through his mind. He crossed the next backstreet, turned left by the brewery into another alley and paused at the entrance into Quay Street.

He checked . . . downhill and up.

It was empty as the other.

But the harbour was nearer.

And the stink of fish stronger than before.

Rick took a chance, ran the last few metres through the soft rain falling, down the basement steps and into the workshop. He was safe then with the door closed behind him, leaning against it, blinking in the harsh electric light. It was a small mean room. Broken shutters were at the windows and its walls were lined with shelves containing bales of cloth. There were sewing machines and tailors' dummies, and a door to a back room where Hannah waited. Hearing him arrive she stepped from the darkness to greet him.

'You're late,' she said.

'I met a robo-cop,' Rick told her.

There was silence and she turned her head.

Haggarty came from the shadows.

'Mackenna?' he asked.

'He didn't introduce himself,' said Rick.

'If Mackenna's got wind . . .'

'I back-tracked,' said Rick. 'He didn't follow.'

'I don't trust that bastard!'

'It mightn't have been him,' said Hannah.

Haggarty scowled at her.

'We can hope!' he said savagely. 'And you should have listened! I told you not to involve a bloody greenhorn! And a West Side kid at that! What does he know about us? And what does he care?'

'He knows *me*,' Hannah said quietly. 'And he cares enough to risk his whole life to come here. Isn't that enough?'

Rick smiled at her.

She was a tall slender girl.

Beautiful with the lamplight shining on her hair.

'I want to help,' he said earnestly.

Haggarty leaned against the door-jamb.

'Why?' He asked pointedly.

'Isn't it obvious?'

'For the girl?' suggested Haggarty.

'Not just for me,' said Hannah. 'Tell him, Rick.'

'That could take all night,' Rick objected.

'I'm in no hurry,' Haggarty said.

Rick tried to explain. He had many reasons and they all began with Hannah, but she was not a reason in herself. She was just a girl he had met at a ball game, a pretty girl with long blond hair who had watched him from the sidelines and whom, afterwards, he had talked to. He had not known who she was, or where she came from, or how she lived . . . until she told him. Then he was appalled. The contrast between her way of life and his own sickened and shamed him. She, and thousands like her, existed in squalor, all of them in the same State, the same city as himself. The realization had made him despise himself and everyone else who was well-fed, well-cared for, well-clad, with money to spare and spend on whatever they wanted to buy. They were all human beings, all passengers on the same planet. Why should some have so much and others have almost nothing? It was social injustice of the worst possible kind and, quite simply, Rick could not live with that kind of knowledge and not do something about it.

'So you want to assuage your own conscience?' concluded Haggarty. 'And your chief motivation is one of guilt?'

'What I feel is anger,' said Rick.

'I told you he was genuine,' Hannah said proudly.

Haggarty ignored her.

'Do you have access to a copying machine?' he asked Rick.

'Several,' said Rick.

'His father works in a bank,' said Hannah.

'I could get you plans of the security system,' offered Rick.

'We could work out a raid,' said Hannah.

'I need to know if I can trust him first,' said Haggarty.

'Of course you can trust him,' Hannah insisted.

'So what do you want copied?' asked Rick.

There was a small pause where he and Hannah waited, and Haggarty summed him up. He could hear the rain tapping softly on the windowpanes and the tick of time on a battery clock above the doorway. Twenty-five past midnight, it said. And Rick was suddenly tired from the tension, wet and cold and wanting to go home.

'Well,' he said. 'If you're not going to use me . . .'

'Hang about,' Haggarty said gruffly.

And he took from his jacket pocket a printed sheet of paper.

'This is a political pamphlet,' he said. 'It's anti-government propaganda and I want five hundred copies. You understand the implications?'

'Yes,' said Rick.

'You're not bound to get involved with us.'

'It's why he came,' Hannah said impatiently.

She took the pamphlet from Haggarty's hand and gave it to Rick. Her eyes shone and her smile made a glow of warmth inside him. He wanted to kiss her, but Haggarty was there and this was a business meeting.

'Five hundred copies,' Rick said softly.

'I'll collect them on Saturday,' said Hannah. 'After the ball game.'

'Take care of yourself.'

'And you,' said Hannah.

She squeezed his arm as he turned to go.

'Just watch your step,' warned Haggarty.

Those were the last words he spoke.

Outside the door the robo-cop hovered.

And Haggarty died from a shot in the brain.

The robo-cop had followed Rick along the alleyways and

141

into Quay Street. There, briefly, Mackenna had lost him, until he remembered the girl. She had closed the shutters but bright chinks of light showed between the broken slats, so presumably she was still there in the basement workshop. And was she still sewing at five minutes to midnight? Mackenna wondered. Or was Rick with her, vanished down the steps and out of sight before the robo-cop rounded the corner?

He sent it to check, had it hover by the window, its lens eyes peering through the cracks. He saw the girl standing at an inner doorway and someone in the darkness beyond her, shadowy and indistinct. He heard the murmur of voices and recognized Rick's. Love's young fool risking his neck for a teenage pash, Mackenna thought mockingly. But it was more than that. Suddenly a man stepped clear into the light. He was red-bearded and unmistakable . . . Jack Haggarty, the political agitator . . . a rat! Mackenna had been after him for months. And the boy was with him, involved in some anti-government plot.

All Mackenna needed was proof. He set the recorders, increased the sound sensitivity and listened. Their conversation left him with no doubt. All three were guilty of conspiracy. His anger rose, lethal and cold. He would teach Rick a lesson he would never forget and Jack Haggarty would die.

One clear shot was all Mackenna needed but the shutters impeded his view. He waited until Rick opened the door. One clear shot . . . and his aim was true. He saw Haggarty fall, heard the girl scream, but failed to enter the room. Rick slammed the robo-cop outside. Miles away Mackenna cursed softly, wished he were there in person, then regained control and had the robo-cop fire the next shot through the window splintering wood and glass. Aimed vaguely it embedded itself in the wall above the girl's head. Again it was Rick who acted, hauled her from the firing line and switched off the light. Then there was silence. Rain trickled from a broken gutter and the wind whined wetly along the street. A few pale faces of people peered from upstairs windows nearby.

Mackenna switched on the hailer.

His voice came loud in the hushed night.

'Come out! Both of you! With your hands up!'

Nothing happened.

Mackenna waited, repeated the order.

Then had the robo-cop blast its way inside.

Haggarty was dead all right, slumped on the floor in a pool of blood, but Rick and the girl had gone. Closed doors slowed the robo-cop's progress as Mackenna searched through empty rooms, along a corridor and out into a concrete yard with sheds and dustbins and a garden beyond. It was gone to wildness but their trail was clear under the spotlight, a trampled path through long grass and brambles and scuff marks of shoes on the wall that flanked the brewery yard. Mackenna's view was impeded by the leaves of an overhanging tree but he sensed they were over there, hiding somewhere among the stacked barrels. He switched off the light and the robo-cop hovered silently as he listened. He heard rain on leaves . . . cats yowling in the distance . . . and softly, distinctly, a girl's stifled sobbing.

'Dead,' she wept

'But we're still alive,' soothed Rick.

'What'll we do?'

'Stay here,' said Rick. 'Wait until the coast is clear.'

'And what then?'

'Make a run for it.'

'Go home you mean? Go our separate ways?'

'No,' said Rick. 'We're in this together so we'll stay together. I won't leave you, Hannah.'

Mackenna smiled and retreated, sent the robo-cop rising and spinning over the side wall of the garden, along the alley and into the backstreet where it lurked and rested, a lump of darkness in the entrance of a disused nightclub. Opposite were the high mesh gates that led from the brewery yard. And with the robo-cop in position Mackenna waited, leaned back in his chair and poured himself a fresh coffee, watched as the vision screens flickered. Twenty minutes passed. He began to wonder if Rick had back-tracked and escaped through the house, but finally he saw him in the lea of the building coming warily to check the street. Nothing moved among the shadows and the lamplight, only the slants of yellow rain still falling.

Thinking it safe, Rick beckoned to Hannah. The gates rattled as they climbed. Mackenna heard the thump of their shoes on the pavement and let them go, running down a distance of the hill, before he had the robo-cop follow. It moved unseen, from doorway to doorway. And they were heading for the harbour, Mackenna thought, but then they turned left towards the railway sidings. He increased the robo-cop's speed, afraid he might lose them among the rabbit-warren of streets, the tatty terraces of houses. Even in daylight it was an unsavoury place to be, most of it derelict and boarded up, inhabited by drunks and drop-outs and drug addicts and other more murderous men. But Hannah obviously lived there, or knew someone else who lived there, for Mackenna saw her pause by a shabby front door and take from her pocket something that might have been a key.

Then he acted. From far behind the robo-cop sped towards them. Its siren wailed and its blue light flashed a warning, instilling fear, urging them to run. It was automatic. Spray flew from their heels as they fled . . . on along the street and under the railway arches, across the sidings, along a concrete dock and into a warehouse. They did not have time to hide. Their footsteps echoed up a stairway, across vast empty floor spaces and storage areas stacked with wooden crates and sacks of grain. Mackenna drove them upwards, higher and higher, until finally on the topmost landing he had them trapped. The fire door failed to open and below the windows was a twenty-metre drop.

'We can't get out!' Rick said desperately.

'Pull down the bar,' urged Hannah.

'It must be jammed or something.'

'We've had it then.'

Unhurriedly the robo-cop approached and she turned to face it. She was breathing hard and soaked to the skin, her fair hair darkened by the rain. But her chin lifted proudly and her blue eyes flashed in defiance as she stared into the spotlight.

'Why don't you kill us?' she cried.

Rick heaved downwards with all his strength.

And the robo-cop closed in on them.

'Why don't you kill us?' Hannah cried.

And someone laughed, softly, a man's voice echoing around the hollow stairwell, as if he was enjoying what he did. But Rick was not ready to die. Desperately he pushed and tugged and, with a sudden click, the door gave way, opened outwards. He pulled Hannah through and closed it behind them, solid metal giving them time. The fire escape clattered as they went down and the wind whistled past them, cold from the sea, full of salt and rain and fishy smells, buffeting darkness whipping the words from their mouths.

'It's useless anyway!' shouted Hannah.

'Nothing's useless!' retorted Rick.

'It'll be there at the bottom before us!'

'Not if we hurry!'

'But what's the point?' shouted Hannah. 'We won't get far and there's nowhere to hide! It'll follow and find us wherever we go so we might as well face it!'

'There's got to be some way!' shouted Rick.

They reached the bottom as the robo-cop rounded the corner. Once again the siren wailed and the blue light flashed. And whatever Hannah said she still ran, following Rick along the length of the quay. He could hear the rasp of her breathing, her footsteps pounding the concrete, sense the strain in her lungs and leg muscles.

Untrained, she could not keep up the pace for very long. And the robo-cop continued to pursue, its light flashing eerily blue, a lethal machine cruising effortlessly behind.

'I've got to rest,' gasped Hannah.

'Not yet,' said Rick.

'We'll never out-run it!'

'I don't intend to,' said Rick.

He gripped her hand and unexpectedly changed course, dodged among the lifting cranes that towered in the darkness over them, stumbled over coiled ropes and pulley chains, ducking beneath gantries and grab-arms where the robo-cop could not go. It had to reverse and find another way. And they were out in the open again then, where railway lines curved among gravel, and he dragged her the last few metres to an abandoned engine shed.

Wind whined through the broken windows and the carcasses of old locomotives lay about, wheels and chassis and defunct carriages, half-remembered from a long ago visit. Now they were just vague black shapes in the darkness and he had to let go of Hannah's hand to feel his way. Broken glass crunched beneath his shoes and paint flaked when he touched it, but he found the footplate, helped Hannah climb inside and in again through the broken wall of the cab. There they sat in the boiler housing among smells of iron and rust, out of sight, out of reach, with the curved wall at their backs and their feet in water. Outside the rain pattered on the roof of the shed, dripped through the slates as they waited.

Half an hour passed.

And the robo-cop did not appear.

'We've lost it,' Rick said thankfully.

'We thought that once before,' Hannah reminded him.

'This time we'll be more patient. We'll wait until morning.'

'It'll still be lurking,' said Hannah.

'*It* is a man,' said Rick. 'He's bound to go off duty sooner or later.'

'*He* is Mackenna!' Hannah said savagely.

'What difference does a name make?' Rick inquired. 'He's still a man. He has a stomach and a bladder and a need to sleep like any other man.'

'He'll see us dead before he ever sleeps,' said Hannah.

Rick closed his eyes.

He had not meant it to be like this, never imagined he would get caught. It had seemed a fine thing to do, a fine thing to get involved in, living for a cause, helping the fight against injustice. He had wanted to become part of the underground movement, help Hannah and Haggarty and others like them redress the balance. But now Haggarty was dead, and Rick was being hunted, and the whole thing was useless. Even if he escaped with his life he was done for. Mackenna would report him. He would be tried for conspiracy and sent to jail. After that no university would ever accept him. Effectively his life was over. He would have no future, no position, no place. He would end up like Hannah in some poky little room in the slum part of town, forced into menial labour or having to exist on Social Security hand-outs, his potential wasted and his intelligence denied. It was better to be dead than live like that, he thought. Better to be dead than bring shame on his family and have to carry the disgrace. Fear lodged like sickness in his stomach.

'Suppose he doesn't intend to kill us?' he said.

'Who?' asked Hannah.

'Mackenna,' said Rick.

'He killed Haggarty, didn't he?'

'That doesn't necessarily mean . . .'

'You don't know him,' Hannah muttered.

'Maybe not,' said Rick. 'But he could have killed us half a hundred times already . . . so why hasn't he?'

'Have you ever seen a cat with a mouse?' asked Hannah.

Rick bit his lip. Water soaked through his shoes and his cold feet cramped. He could feel Hannah soaked and shivering beside him. He wanted to warm her, comfort

147

her, but he did not know how any more, was unable to cross the great divide of his own thoughts, his own self-concern. It was as if Mackenna had driven a wedge between them, separated them forever although they sat there together. Time dragged. There was nothing to do, nothing to see, and the darkness grew icy. If they stayed there much longer they would probably die of pneumonia anyway, thought Rick.

'We could give ourselves up,' he suggested.

'We can't do that!' said Hannah.

'Why not? We have to face it sooner or later . . . you said that.'

'I meant death, not defeat,' said Hannah.

'What's the difference? We're dead either way.'

'If I die,' Hannah said sharply, 'it will be Mackenna's crime, not mine. I may get shot in the back but I won't surrender.'

'You just want to be a sodding martyr!' said Rick.

She shrugged.

And they waited.

It was all right for her, he thought bitterly. At least she had lived for a reason and would die trying. Her death would be a noble thing, a young girl defying the tyranny of the State. But his would be an act of stupidity, a waste of his life because he had done nothing with it. Dead or alive then he had nothing to hope for. Unless he could do a deal with Mackenna? Come to some arrangement?

Rick pondered the possibility.

He was useless to Hannah.

But if he gave Mackenna certain information . . .

'There's no point in staying here,' he said.

'Well, we can hardly go out there,' said Hannah.

'I'm willing to risk it,' said Rick.

'And what about me?' she demanded.

'It's up to you,' said Rick. 'You're welcome to come with me.'

'I can't do that! It's betraying everything I believe in! Stay with me, Rick. Please stay with me. We'll work something out. We could run away together . . . go to another State . . . another country . . . work in the fields.'

But Rick would not listen to her, not any more. Loving her had no place in all this, nor caring either. He had his own life to think of and her touch irritated, her hand on his sleeve, holding him back. He shook himself free and crawled through the gap. Grey dawn showed beyond the broken windows of the engine shed and the rain had stopped. His voice echoed loudly as he headed for the doorway.

'Don't shoot, Mackenna! I'm coming out!'

High among the jibs of cranes the robo-cop hovered, watching the entrance to the engine shed and the area around it, clear to the railway sidings in the distance and the warehouses nearby. Had Rick or Hannah made a run for it, Mackenna would have seen them . . . infra-red movements on the vision screen. But they stayed where they were, where the heat detector had located them, warm yellow masses in the boiler housing of an ancient locomotive.

Mackenna relaxed with his feet propped on the desk, ate sandwiches and read a newspaper. After a couple of hours the rain stopped. Grey murky dawn streaked the far horizon and the fishing fleet docked to unload its catch. It was 06.30 hours when finally Rick called to him.

'Don't shoot, Mackenna! I'm coming out!'

Quickly Mackenna cleared his desk, dumped sandwich wrappers, newspaper and plastic cups into the waste bin, and sent the robo-cop to meet him. It had been a long night for all of them and he noted the effects . . . the dirt on Rick's clothes, the pallor of his face, evidence of chill and fear and exposure, and rings of tiredness around his eyes. Without being told to he raised his hands.

'Had enough?' Mackenna inquired.

'Yes,' Rick said quietly.

'Where's the girl?'

'She's still inside.'

'Tell her to come out,' Mackenna instructed.

'She won't,' said Rick.

'Tell her!' Mackenna repeated.

Rick turned and shouted.

'Hannah! You're to come out here!'

'Go to hell!' she replied.

'You see?' Rick said to Mackenna.

Mackenna smiled to himself.

'Looks like it's over between you,' he remarked. 'And was it worth it? All this for a cheap screw?'

'It wasn't like that!' Rick said hotly.

'No?' said Mackenna. 'What was it like then?'

Rick shrugged.

'It doesn't matter, does it? Not any more.'

'And the girl?' asked Mackenna.

'She doesn't matter either,' Rick said dully.

'Her full name?' Mackenna inquired.

'Hannah Pikoulis.'

Mackenna nodded.

He had seen it before . . . idealism gone sour in the face of reality, love turning to indifference. Whatever Rick's motive he had too much to lose . . . possessions, status, future prospects, a place in university. He would not willingly give up the easy life to share in Hannah's human squalor, her struggle for existence, her futile fight against the State. A taste of death, a dose of distress, a night on the run and a glimpse of his own ruination, was all he had needed. He would do anything now, anything to turn back the clock and wipe clean his record . . . deny, betray or kill. Or would he?

Mackenna needed to find out.

'Hannah Pikoulis is a revolutionary!' he said curtly. 'She is a contagion to society along with all her kind. The State will want rid of her and I certainly don't want her operating on my patch. We'll make it an accident, I think. You'll find a can of paraffin and a storm lantern in the warehouse . . . go and fetch it.'

Rick stared at the robo-cop.

'What are you suggesting.'

'A favour for a favour?' Mackenna said softly.

There was a long silence.

Rain dripped from the overhead wires and a small wind ruffled Rick's hair. The sea fog swirled about him. And just for a moment Mackenna thought he might comply, that when it came to safeguarding his future and his rich way of life, he would even commit murder. Then there were shouts in the distance of men unloading fish boxes on the quay, sounds of humanity, and herring gulls screaming and a single slant of sun. Rick's face twisted. His eyes flashed, and his fists clenched at his side, and his voice came harsh and hating.

'In Hannah's words, Mackenna, it will be your crime, not mine, if she dies!'

He turned on his heel and walked away. He felt emptied of emotion, incapable of feeling, and he had no delusions about himself. Women arriving at the fish factory bellowed their greetings and early morning trains shunted from the sidings. What would happen to Rick and Hannah was left for Mackenna to decide. And Mackenna was State Police, licensed to kill, a man with a job to do. He was not paid to hold opinions, or care. With one swift movement he wiped clean the computer. Nothing remained of the night's happenings . . . only the body of Jack Haggarty in a basement workshop on Quay Street and a memory in three human minds.

7

Rigel Light

Rigel is the brightest star in the constellation of Orion, a vast blue binary sun with planets revolving around it . . . and on the third planet of its solar system Maggie was born. Her home was an isolated farming complex in the foothills of the Indigo Mountains where Jessica, her mother, worked as a bio-technician along with Ed Barnes and the others who shared the communal living quarters. They were employed by the Galactic Mining Company to produce Earth-type foods for the various mining settlements scattered around the planet.

Humid and forested, plagued by electrical storms and only partially explored, Rigel Three was hardly suitable for colonization. But it was rich in minerals and metal ores and the Mining Company paid high wages to anyone willing to work there. They even accepted Jessica, large with child in the months before Maggie was born, although they provided no facilities for children. Her nursery had been the acres of glass-houses and the open fields of soya beans, sweet corn and cabbage. And baby-minders varied with the duty rota . . . Brian or Sarah, Ritchie or Sue or, best of all, Ed Barnes.

From the moment Maggie could toddle she latched on to Ed. He was rough Australian and called her the nipper. He gave her shoulder rides, told her fairy stories, answered her questions and dandled her on his knee. He watched her grow, the only youngster among half a dozen adults who had neither the time nor the inclination to pay her much attention. And the native field-hands were born without vocal chords, speechless menials who were not much company for a human child. Left to her own devices Maggie chattered to herself, invented solitary games, ran wild and unsupervised under the blue heat of the sun. And once, when the gates were opened and the produce truck left for the nearest mining settlement, she went exploring.

Her child's mind admitted no fear among the great dark trees beyond the perimeter fences. The jungle sang to her with its unseen choirs of insects and birds, a world of blue diffuse light and sapphire shadows. She climbed towards the high silence of the hills, to the sacred burial grounds where the spirits lived that ate the bodies of the native dead. And there, across the final openness where the jungle ended and the mountains rose towards the sky, she saw the flame people dancing. Spellbound, Maggie watched them, living forms that were veiled in tongues of pale fire. And the landscape shimmered around her in indescribable shades of mauve and violet with the forest growing inky behind her as the great sun set. Long shadows fell across the blue-grass ridges.

There were voices then, human voices howling for her to come home, transmitting their terror. Beautiful and dancing the flame people came drifting towards her but Maggie screamed and fled. She tried to tell Ed . . . fire fairies, she said. But he spanked her around the legs and Jessica sent her to bed.

'Don't ever go outside the gates again!' Jessica said.

As Maggie grew older she forgot about the flame people. There were other things to occupy her mind. Even on outback planets education was compulsory. During the evening darkness, when colours were strange and harsh beneath the yellow inside light, Jessica and Ritchie taught her to read and write and Brian taught her basic mathematics. Later the video-machine took over. For hours each day she was locked inside with its flickering screen as the strawberries flowered and the bean fields smelled sweet at the start of the short dry summer season. Rigelian field hands moved among the raspberry canes, their pale young faces streaked with dirt and sweat. Mute and motherless and little more than children, they lived for only seven years and worked from dawn to dusk for no wages. But to Maggie they retained a freedom she had lost and sometimes she wished she had been born Rigelian.

'You've got to stay inside and learn!' Ed Barnes told her.

But more often than not Maggie was gone . . . a bare-footed girl, wilful and undisciplined, hiding among acres of blossoming beans. She ate strawberries and carrots and raw peas, whatever crop was in season, and did not return until twilight.

Then the fear began for those who had come from Earth. The fence wires hummed and sparked with high voltage electricity and pale points of fire flickered across the lower slopes of the Indigo Mountains. They were the Rigel Lights, Ed told her . . . will-o'-the-wisps or Saint Elmo's fires. And down in the graveyard by the pumpkin patch five men were buried who had died from the madness those lights made. They get inside your head, Ed said. But the fences kept them out and it was never Maggie's fear.

For her the Rigel Lights were always beautiful. She could watch them for hours, delicate and dancing, rainbow spots of colour in the midnight blue distance coming nearer and nearer. It never occurred to her they might attack. But Brian talked of ghouls and Sarah feared them and many a time Jessica came screaming across the darkening fields to haul Maggie inside.

'How many times do I have to tell you!' Jessica shouted. 'When you see those things around you're to stay in the house!'

'The kid wants taking in hand,' Ed said.

'Someone to keep a permanent eye on her,' said Sarah.

'Yesterday,' said Ritchie, 'I caught her fiddling with the gate controls. And someone turned the sprinklers on full in number three glass-house.'

'I don't have eyes in the back of my head!' Jessica said.

'She'll grow up to be educationally backward,' said Sue. 'That's three times this week she's dodged lessons. You're going to have to get a minder for her.'

'Those Rigelians give me the creeps!' Jessica said.

'But we're thinking of Maggie, not you,' said Ed.

Maggie watched him hatch from the egg, a vague pink shape the size of a human baby. A month before, when she had come with Ed to order him, the sensors had sexed him as a female. But the newly emerged mind made its own decision. Fluid and sticky, the shape budded arms and legs and male appendages and Maggie watched in total fascination until Jessica caught her hand and pulled her away.

'We ordered a female,' Jessica said primly.

'Mistakes do happen,' said the incubation assistant.

'Do you have another?' Jessica asked.

'I don't want another!' Maggie wailed. 'I want that one! It was my egg he came out of! I chose it! Ed said I could!'

'And there are no others,' said the incubation assistant.

Jessica glanced around the hatchery.

There must have been hundreds.

Rigelians failed to breed in captivity, failed even to reach maturity during their short seven years of life. The eggs were laid by wild Rigelians, great abandoned clutches in remote parts of the planet that were carefully gathered and brought to the hatchery. Everywhere in the battery-heated cots the white shells cracked and split under the hot lights, poured out their pink amorphous blobs of life.

It was the first time Jessica had visited the hatchery . . . the first time she had witnessed the birth of these alien

155

things. Hard to believe that in three months' time these shapeless maggoty babies would be fully grown into the black-haired child-people of Rigel Three, ready to work in the fields or down the mines, replacing those who were due to die in the autumn. And hard to believe that the changeling boy whom Jessica was so loath to accept would become a minder for her own daughter.

'The psycho-emotional read-outs show no distinction between the Rigelian sexes,' the incubation assistant informed her. 'I can assure you that after undergoing the statutory training the boy will prove perfectly suitable.'

'And I do want him!' Maggie sobbed. 'Ed said he was mine!'

Jessica sighed.

She returned to lean above the cot and the coal-black eyes of the alien child seemed to fix on her face. They saw too much, understood too much, and she feared the silence of the mind that was behind them. The blackness glittered and Jessica shuddered. After eight years she ought to be used to it . . . the eerie haunted atmosphere of the blue planet . . . those black Rigelian eyes and dumb silences . . . but she knew she would never feel easy with him around the house. But Maggie wept for him, wanted him, a pink baby thing, newborn and defenceless. Maggie did not understand . . . a few hours from now he would clutch his first fruit and feed himself . . . and tomorrow he would take his first step.

Yet for Maggie's sake Jessica was bound to own him. She bent to comfort.

'What will you call him?' she asked.

Before Maggie left the hatchery she named him Kirk, after the starship captain on an antique video-show. He was delivered to the farming complex a week before the autumn rains began along with the replacement field-hands. Like them he was tall and bony with black curling hair and smouldering eyes. On the human age scale he looked maybe fifteen years old and eight-year-old

Maggie gazed at him in awe. He was not as she expected, not the Kirk of her imagination who had shared her life these past weeks and become her friend. He was dour and silent . . . a total stranger. Disappointment and anger mixed with Maggie's shyness and she clung to Ed's hand whilst Sarah showed him around.

He would sleep with the field-hands in the outside chalets but the rest of the time he would spend with Maggie and take his meals in the communal kitchen . . . like one of the family, Sarah said. And video-lessons, Sarah informed him, lasted from 09.00 hours to 16.30 and supper was served at 18.15. He was to ensure that Maggie appeared regularly for both.

Kirk nodded his head in understanding. Like the rest of his kind his obedience was perfect and there was no question of anyone not trusting him. He had been taught to fear the Rigel Lights as much as humans did and Brian showed him how to operate the gate controls and switch on the voltage if under attack. He was given the key to the video-room and a whistle to summon help in case of fire, or accident, or trouble with Maggie.

'And that's all there is to it,' Sarah said.

'We hope you'll be happy here,' said Brian.

Ed rested his hand on Kirk's shoulder.

'We're not expecting miracles,' Ed said. 'Just do your best, son, that's all we ask. And you behave yourself!' he said to Maggie.

Deep inside the resentment began.

And everyone watched to see what Kirk would do and how she reacted. He spelled out his message in simple sign language which Maggie could not fail to understand and held out his hand for her to accompany him into the video-room. On the blind side of Ed, Maggie stuck out her tongue. Nothing showed on Kirk's face, no anger, no response . . . but his dark eyes seemed to bore into her brain, a compelling blackness from which she could not look away. It was as if he touched her deep inside, soft and fluttering, sifting through every nerve of her body, searching for something and finding nothing but hostility. He understood and the blackness glittered as he pointed to the door a second time, then clenched his fist to show that something very nasty might happen to her if she did not obey.

Ed laughed.

Rigelians were non-aggressive.

But Kirk had been trained to use human gestures.

And he needed human support.

'Best do what he says, little lady,' Ed said.

'Unless you want a tanned backside,' said Sarah.

Maggie went, muttering in her mind, mean nasty feelings simmering below the surface. They were all on Kirk's side now . . . even Ed . . . and there was no one left for Maggie. It was his fault. She would make him sorry he had ever come here! She would make him wish he had never hatched from the egg!

Maggie set out to be deliberately difficult, a bane to Kirk in every possible way. She knew the rules about not touching the video-controls but she altered them all and put the blame on him. Colours pulsed in lurid green and purple. Voices gabbled, jammed at full speed and the computer link-up broke. It took Brian three days to fix it and Kirk bore the brunt of his temper. Then, twice in one day, Maggie had him unlock the video-room door for her to use the lavatory only to run away. It was uncanny how quickly he found where she was hiding but there was no way he could make her return to the house units without using physical force. All he could do was blow the emergency whistle and wait for someone to come.

'My patience is beginning to wear very thin,' Jessica said.

Then the rains began.

And the field-hands started to sicken.

Ritchie, who was the base medic, could do nothing to save them. Nine died within a week and during that week, as if they were attracted by the scent of death, the

Rigel Lights attacked. All night Maggie watched them, bolts of rainbow fire that hurled themselves at the fence wire only to recoil and try again, or explode in a shower of coloured sparks. Laser beams blasted away the darkness as Ed and Brian fought. Jessica, savage with fear, used a primitive flame gun and Sue worked on the back-up generator to boost the fluctuating power.

And all the while the rain poured down.

It rained for three successive days and nights and for three successive nights the Rigel Lights attacked. But finally, when the last field-hand died, they went away . . . diminished into distance until they appeared no more than fallen stars twinkling against the blue-velvet backdrop of the mountains. In sodden dawn the burial parties toiled up the jungle track to the sacred burial ground.

Kirk bent his head as they passed.

It was his first experience of death.

Bodies being buried in black earth.

'The worms eat them,' Maggie told him. 'And Ritchie says the Rigel Lights feed off all the smelly gases. And that's what will happen to you in seven years' time.' And she saw in the black depths of his eyes a little flicker of fear.

Autumn was never an easy time at the farming complex. The Rigelian deaths left their mark, their losses felt even in human hearts after a seven-year acquaintance. The new field-hands had yet to learn the routine and the weather alternated between breathless heat and violent thunderstorms. Number five glass-house shattered in a freak wind and a thousand young cabbage plants were washed from the ground. Human tempers frayed around the edges. They seemed to move in a miasma of mud and dampness, a blue gloom, sodden and inescapable. And this was the time Maggie chose to be difficult. This was the time she forced Kirk to blow his whistle . . . again and again and again. Tramping down through two fields of battered blueberries Jessica blew her top.

'I'm sick of you two!' Jessica screamed. 'There's an ore freighter leaving next month,' she said to Maggie. 'And you're going to be on it! You can go to boarding school back on Earth! And as for you,' she said to Kirk. 'For all the use you are as a child-minder you might as well go join the field-hands! Now both of you . . . clear off back to the video-room!'

All the way back to the house units Jessica's words howled in Maggie's head, a tirade of anger that went on and on. And the spaceship to Earth was the ultimate threat, the ultimate rejection. And maybe Kirk sensed the fear she felt for he held out his hand as if to touch her, a gesture of compassion in the silence. But it was he who had blown the whistle. It was his fault Jessica would send her away, billions of miles to an unknown Earth. Her face twisted in a monstrous anger and she kicked him hard on the shin.

It was as if something struck her, a slap inside her head that sent her reeling. She fell against the opposite wall, cowered in the corner by the video-machine and covered her head with her arms to try and ward off the blows. But the pain went on . . . the cuff of Kirk's hand against her mind as his voice battered her.

'Stupid! Vicious! Ignorant Maggie! What good has it done you? What have you gained from tormenting me? Nothing! You're alone like you never were before! And how does it feel to be hurt, and hated and not wanted? How do you think I've felt? Now you pay for it, Maggie!'

'No!' Maggie whimpered. 'Not any more! Don't hit me any more!'

The hurting stopped.

'We could have been friends,' Kirk said. 'Both of us together. I came here for you. I wanted to like you.' He gripped her wrists. 'It's not too late,' he said. 'If we work together . . . if we make up for these past weeks your mother might not send you away. You've got to try, Maggie. You can't grow up to be stupid and mindless and vicious. Don't you want to learn about the world you

160

came from? Don't you want to learn about plants and stars and chemistry?'

Maggie stared at him.

Soft black eyes seen blurred through her tears.

'You can talk!' she said wonderingly.

'No . . . you can listen,' he said.

And she realized then that his voice was silent.

That she heard him only in her heart and in her head.

Jessica did not send Maggie away on the Earth-bound freighter, nor was Kirk sent from the house to join the field-hands. Suddenly they began to work together. And not only did they run through the scheduled video-lessons . . . they also began to use the micro-library stored in the computer. Learning absorbed them and they troubled no one. But Ed sensed the strange affinity that lay between them . . . companions in adversity and more than that . . . with Maggie, Kirk no longer used sign language. Indeed it was uncanny the way Maggie interpreted his dumbness, the way she laughed and spoke to him and even argued . . . as if the silence brimmed with the unheard things he said. Ed was convinced Kirk talked to her.

'You mean telepathic communication?' Ritchie said.

'It wouldn't surprise me where Rigelians are concerned,' said Sue. 'But Maggie's human.'

'She's a nipper,' said Ed. 'Nippers have strange ways of knowing.'

'If it's true,' said Ritchie. 'And Kirk is communicating with her . . . Jessica's not going to like it.'

'Do we have to tell her?' Ed said. 'Where's the harm in it, I say? They're both of them nippers and Maggie needs a friend.'

'We don't *have* to tell her,' Ritchie said dubiously.

'And there are none so blind as those who will not see,' said Sue. 'Jessica will come to it in her own sweet time without any help from us.'

So the years passed.

During the two following autumns when the field-hands died the Rigel Lights attacked again . . . but then, for some unknown reason, they withdrew altogether from the nearby ridges, drifting so far away among the mountains that even the fear of them was gone. Humans slept easy in their beds and during the day the gates were left open. For the first time in her life Maggie was free to come and go. And Jessica saw only what she wanted to see . . . an ordinary little girl with Kirk in charge of her, skipping beside him up the jungle track . . . a child chasing butterflies across the sacred burial grounds or paddling in pools below cliffs that were purple as plums in the blue afternoon light.

Blue summer followed blue summer and Jessica never dreamed of what would come. Sometimes Maggie's intense enigmatic conversations with no one in particular puzzled her . . . and sometimes Kirk's eyes across the supper table scared her with their intimations of intelligence . . . but mostly Jessica failed to notice what Ed and Sue, Ritchie and Sarah, saw quite clearly and Brian automatically accepted. Brian had always known how deeply Kirk and Maggie were involved. In overall charge of the computer, he knew what video-lessons were being run through and had followed their development. It was as if they were searching for something . . . the meaning of existence perhaps.

'They're into quantum physics and applied theology now!' Brian said.

'Who are?' Jessica asked him.

'Maggie and Kirk,' he said.

'Don't be absurd,' said Jessica. 'He's just a dumb Rigelian and she's no more than a child.'

'Dumb?' said Brian. 'He's about as dumb as Einstein was and Maggie's not far behind. We may credit Rigelians with no more than primitive intelligence but in this case we were wrong. And I don't know where you've been these last six years Jessica, but at fourteen you can hardly call Maggie a child. She and Kirk are pretty close, you know. The original beautiful relationship, I'd say. Hadn't you noticed?'

Jessica stared at him.

She could not believe what he said.

She did not want to believe . . . but Brian nodded towards the window and she was bound to look. In the sapphire twilight Jessica saw them walking with Ed along the avenue of glass-houses . . . a girl on the threshold of womanhood and a young man with dark curling hair. She saw how they laughed at something Ed said, then smiled at each other. She saw how their hands touched and held. Jessica clenched her fists. The shock of realization turned to anger.

'How long has this been going on?' Jessica screamed.

The farmstead turned wild.

Kirk was banished from the house to live among the field-hands and Maggie was sent to her room, forbidden ever to see him again. And finally Jessica turned on Ed.

'You knew all along, didn't you?' Jessica shouted.

'Maybe I did,' said Ed. 'But it was always too late.'

'What do you mean . . . too late?' Jessica said savagely. 'He's a damn blasted alien, Ed! What the hell are you thinking of?'

'I'm thinking they love each other,' Ed said quietly. 'And I'm thinking there's nothing you, or I, or anyone else can do about it because in six months' time he'll be dead.'

Pumpkin flowers bloomed palely in the blue dawn light and the human graveyard was white with starry blossoms. Maggie was not unaware of the irony of the place, the carved headstones symbolizing death in the midst of burgeoning life. Rain dripped from the overhead trees and Kirk leaned against the picket fence and brooded. His shirt was soaked, as if he had been standing there all night.

'Jessica sent me,' Maggie said. 'You're to come to the house for breakfast, she says.'

'Last night,' said Kirk, 'she told me never to darken her doors again!'

'And now she's prepared to apologize,' said Maggie.

Kirk's voice came mocking into her mind.

'Apologize to a slave? That's big of her.'

'You're not a slave!' Maggie objected.

'Don't be naive,' he replied. 'All Rigelians are slaves. We accepted that long ago so why deny it now?'

'Ed made it all right for us anyway,' Maggie muttered.

'I suppose he pointed out that she needed only turn a blind eye for another six months before I do her a favour and drop dead?' Kirk said.

'That's horrible!' Maggie said tearfully.

'It's true!' Kirk said bitterly. 'We've run out of time, haven't we? Your mother should have stuck to what she said and made you stay away from me! Have you thought what it will be like for you, Maggie . . . watching me . . . waiting . . . knowing. I don't feel very brave. There's this godawful . . .'

He bit his lip.

Fear, thought Maggie.

He was afraid of death, the black termination, although he had always lived with the prospect just as she had done. But somehow it had always been in the future. Now the years had drained away and he stood on the edge of the last blue summer and finally faced it . . . the ultimate terror. And she stood beside him, equally afraid . . . afraid of the loneliness when he was gone, the terrible grief and a lifetime unbearable without him. She touched his arm, trying to comfort him but needing comfort herself.

He pointed to the gravestones.

'They were lucky,' he said.

'They died of the Rigel Lights,' said Maggie.

'But they didn't know they were going to,' Kirk said. 'They didn't know they would end when they had hardly begun to live. We've failed, Maggie. We've failed to find a meaning. Quantum physics or Wordsworth's poetry . . . it doesn't matter how many intimations of immortality we find. In the end the fear remains that there really is nothing. It's all been wasted, Maggie! I'm just a lump of worm meat . . . a source of methane for the Rigel Lights. Every breath I've taken has been totally and absolutely meaningless.'

Maggie shook her head.

'You mean something to me,' she said.

'And you won't be there,' he said. 'Not where I'm going.'

'I will one day,' she told him.

'Bones beside me in the black earth?' he asked.

Maggie shrugged.

'I want to be buried here,' he said.

Towards the end of the summer the Rigel Lights returned, lurked on the ridge above the farming complex as if they were waiting . . . death birds hovering on wings of fire, silent and menacing. Daylight dissolved them but every twilight they drew nearer, a flutter of rainbow fires among the trees exuding their eerie atmospheres. Maggie was always immune to the spooky feelings but they made the hairs stand up on the back of Brian's neck and sent shivers down Sarah's spine.

'What attracts them to us?' Jessica asked.

'Our fear?' said Ritchie.

'Or the prospect of carrion?' said Brian.

'Me!' Kirk said silently.

'No!' said Maggie.

But his death was inevitable.

Autumn storms made a premature darkness . . . the sky growing inky above the Indigo Mountains. In sultry heat the rain sluiced down and five field-hands sickened. Then it was Kirk's turn. All of a sudden he seemed gripped by an overwhelming lassitude and Maggie saw the spores on his skin start to sprout, branching mycelia of a mould that would finally cover him completely in a white cobwebby shroud and harden like bone.

Death came quickly for Rigelians, between one dawn and the next. But in the small stuffy chalet on the edge of the blueberry fields Kirk resisted it. Maggie could feel his fear in her heart, his screams in her head growing fainter and fainter. She tried to tear away the cobweb strands that covered his nose and mouth, the silken suffocating cocoon that Ritchie refused to surgically remove.

'It does no good,' Sarah explained. 'We've tried before and it's kinder to leave it.'

'We can't just do nothing!' Maggie wept.

'Take her out of here,' Ritchie told Sarah.

The woman's warm arms led her away.

Into a kind of madness.

She stood unmoving in the mud and rain, hearing the shriek of human voices, seeing the darkness pulse and flash with lights and laser beams. In a massed attack the flames battered the gates . . . blue and purple, crimson and emerald, rose-gold and brimstone yellow . . . desperate and dangerous. They get inside your head, Ed said . . . just like Kirk had gotten inside Maggie's. But this was a crazy babble . . . beings howling in anger and anguish, demanding to be let in.

The flame people!

Some latent memory flickered and died. Through a blur of tears and rain Maggie saw the stark silhouette of Sue, her hand reaching briefly towards the gate controls in the moment before she died . . . shot in the back by Brian's laser gun. And not only for Kirk did Maggie grieve in the soaking blue stillness of the following morning.

True to his wish Kirk was buried in the human graveyard next to Sue. Mud and rain of winter washed away the flowers and Maggie had never felt so alone. Her sense of loss was almost unbearable. Kirk was gone forever. She would never again hear his voice in her mind, feel his dark gaze touch her and his laughter spin through her veins. He had been so much a part of her she thought she was dying too.

Jessica was not devoid of understanding. She knew the hollow hopeless feelings left behind when some beloved person went for good, be it through death or desertion. It was the loss of Maggie's father that had brought Jessica to Rigel Three in the first place. And that was why she suggested Maggie should go . . . to Earth, with Brian who had terminated his contract with the Galactic Mining Company and would leave after serving out his notice.

'You have to think of your future,' Jessica said.

'I reckon she's right there, girlie,' Ed said kindly. 'Time and distance will take away the pain, you see if it don't. And you can't stay here on this godforsaken planet for the rest of your life.'

But Maggie had been born and brought up on that blue drenched world. It was the only home she had ever known and everything she loved lay buried there. But with Kirk dead there was nothing to keep her . . . only a headstone in the graveyard carved with his name . . . only a memory that eluded her, scraps of knowledge that she failed to understand.

Daily in the blue spring rain when the jungle steamed with heat and the mountains were veiled in drifts of sapphire cloud, Maggie trekked down through the blueberry fields to stand by his grave. It was a compulsion that grew stronger as the days dried and drifted towards summer. Sometimes she would lean against the picket fence for hours without knowing why. A morbid preoccupation, Ritchie called it, and Jessica made the final arrangements for her departure.

'Maybe I don't want to go,' Maggie said doubtfully.

'It's the best thing for you,' Jessica said firmly. 'The dead are dead and it does you no good to brood.'

But it was not something dead Maggie sensed in the graveyard. It was something alive and sleeping, like a root tuber buried in earth. The spring rain disturbed it. The sunlight coaxed it awake. And Maggie waited for it to hatch from the soil . . . something other than flowers.

Deep blue twilight settled over the land, an intense birdless silence broken only by Ed who come to fetch her for supper.

'I'm not hungry,' Maggie said.

'Come back to the house units anyway,' Ed said.

'Not yet,' she replied.

'The Rigel Lights are about,' Ed warned her.

'I know,' said Maggie. 'And they're only interested in the burying grounds, not me.'

'You're not thinking of staying out here all night, are you?' Ed asked her.

'No,' said Maggie. 'Not all night.' She gripped his arm. 'It's starting to happen,' she said. 'Look over there.'

Kirk . . . rest in peace, the headstone said.

And Ed was rooted to the spot.

He saw the earth heave up, split in a black crack. Fingers of fire licked at the edges of the open grave, and down inside a hellish blood-red light pulsed like a heartbeat, paused for a moment then poured itself out. Crumpled and shapeless, like a newly emerged butterfly, it lay inert on the ground, resting as the darkness deepened around it and Maggie held her breath. Ed's voice reached her as a cracked whisper.

'Run up to the house units and get my laser gun,' Ed said.

'What for?' Maggie asked him.

'It's a blasted Rigel Light!' he said.

'It's not hurting *you*!' said Maggie.

'You know what they do!' Ed said urgently.

'They get inside your head,' Maggie quoted.

'And they make you do things you didn't ought to do,' said Ed. 'Sue died because of them. Now go get that gun before the bloody thing moves!'

'It's not doing anything!' Maggie repeated. 'And Sue died because Brian shot her!'

'She would have opened the gates!' said Ed.

And let them in, thought Maggie.

The flame people.

Finally she understood.

'And so did Sue,' Maggie murmured. 'She understood and had pity.'

'What are you talking about?' Ed asked her.

'Flame people!' Maggie said. 'Rigelians! That's what they are in their adult form . . . Rigel Lights. And we steal their eggs and use their children as slaves! And we let those children believe they will die at the end of seven years! They've hardly begun to live and we make them face termination. Think of it, Ed . . . all that fear . . . all those meaningless, loveless childhoods! We don't hear them screaming but their parents do. If we are attacked by the Rigel Lights it's our own fault . . . a natural parental response . . . the desire to reach their children . . . to hold them, comfort them, teach. For them death isn't death, it's metamorphosis. And sometimes I'm ashamed I belong to the human race.'

She turned on her heel and walked towards it . . .

A human girl and a Rigel Light . . .

A flame person, she said.

Ed's thoughts were reeling. It was all too much for him to take in . . . a life cycle that crossed the boundaries between mind and matter . . . beings of light, nebulous and insubstantial, who gave birth to eggs that hatched into flesh-and-blood children, who died and pupated and changed into light. Flame people . . . Ed could not believe it. He could not believe that shapeless blob of luminosity was sentient, capable of thought or feeling or compassion. He watched it rise . . . a pillar of silvery white brightness trailing its tongues of crimson fire. It was taller than he was . . . terrible, beautiful . . . an awesome powerful thing. He wanted to scream . . . 'Come away from it, Maggie!' . . . but she held out her hands to the crimson bright burning and her eyes shone with a strange kind of happiness.

'Hello, Kirk,' Maggie said. 'Welcome back to my head.'

8

All is One

She was one among many wakened by birds carolling in
sunlight, the first magical gleams of a new day. She
sensed somehow it was going to be different, that the sky
glimpsed above the trees contained a secret travelling
towards her, a vision of silver streaking through blue, a
star-sent thing. All sensed it would come, old and
young, from the dark outer reaches of the galaxy of
which they could only dream. Little thrills of excitement
tingled in their nerves, leapt in their hearts' blood and
heightened to gladness. Anticipation changed their
perception of things. And she was one of them, seeing
with delight. Leaves were more verdant, vine flowers
more perfectly white. The forest seemed to sing around
her, myriad life forms mingling in a potency of
existence. She was part of that too, a daughter of the
black earth mothering all things, feeling the earliness of
time.

The star-ones were older, beings from other worlds
who would bring them knowledge. She longed for the
naming of things and her own growing. Yet it could wait.
Her own life was now. She had only to yawn away the
night's sleep and stretch out her limbs to the morning.
Shrill voices called and she rose from her bed, went with
the rest of them, leapt among shadows and dived into
dark pools, shook herself dry in a shower of crystal
drops. And again in the air she felt the imminence of a
thing, saw in her mind's eye silver suspended among

fire. Then she forgot, lingered lovingly by a berry bush and fed on its fruits. Blue juices were sweet on her tongue. And the trees shivered around her in the first slow warming of the sun. She knew them all, and every plant that grew . . . the taste of their roots and seeds and sap. Dark soil trickled through her fingers and she dug. She knew that too, and all its scuttling life. She was akin to the bird that sang in the fern brake, the butterfly that balanced on a scarlet trumpet flower, the tiny golden frog in its pool of nectar gazing up at her with minute exquisite eyes.

And there were nuts growing nearby. She gathered a fistful, carried them to the water's edge and cracked them with a stone. Rainbow fish swam in the shadows, flickered through the reflections of her face, her strange familiar face with yellow slanty eyes and tawny fur. She stared intently, trying to understand what she was, separate and apart from the others. Then, from deep in the forest, she heard the cry of the beast and realized she was alone.

Quick, sharp, the fear froze her. One alone was weak and vulnerable, liable to be hunted as prey and torn apart. But together they were strong. All protected each other and the fanged-one would not attack. She needed to be with many, not by herself.

She was running then, following the scent of their footsteps along the winding path, leaping through glade and thicket, out of shade and into sunlight. She was safer there on the edge of the open plain. Head-high grass swayed dry and feathery, and the wind came singing across it, and she could see the others bounding ahead, joyously, and heedless of her. She could understand why. On the far horizon the ship came down, silver and beautiful in the summer blue sky, its wings screaming with sound and fire. They ran to greet it, all and one, although she was a long way behind.

Only her thoughts cried out to them.

'Wait for me!'

171

Jem fastened his safety harness, gritted his teeth against the G-force as the ship went down. It was a small antiquated cargo vessel and it stank, as Medoc stank, of rotting flesh, dried blood and skins curing in the hold, a miasma of death. Impossible to escape from it, or from Medoc. Merciless hands wrestled with the controls. And soon he would go hunting, bring back the carcasses for Jem to skin and burn.

There was no skill attached to Medoc's trade, no reverence. He used a repeater rifle, travelled from planet to planet wiping out whole herds. He paid no heed to the continuation of species or the Federation culling licence that set a quota. Medoc's chief motivation was greed, or maybe he liked what he did, enjoyed bloodshed. For him an animal had only two values, meat and money. So he killed and ate with a kind of relish, a manic concentration, letting nothing escape, only the waste and the excess . . . entrails and viscera which he threw on the floor, and the grease he wiped on his sleeve. They had meat for every meal . . . rump steaks fried over an open fire, skewered and spit roast or baked in foil, or stewed or microwaved on board the ship. Sometimes the very smell of it made Jem feel sick.

He wished he had never visited Beldia, never been lured to its markets and trading centres and glittering leisure complexes. It was there he had run into Medoc and entered his employ. It had seemed a good idea at the time, one way of travelling the universe, the outback planets far from the main flight paths. Jem had needed a job and Medoc appeared a generous, rollicking man. But the reality was different. All Jem ever saw of other worlds were the blood-stained landing places and Medoc, in truth, was more of a beast than any of the beasts he slaughtered.

Closeted together on board the ship during long inter-planetary flights, Jem had grown to detest him . . . the smell of his breath, the stench of his clothes, his uncouth habits. And the feelings were mutual. Big-bellied, bearded and brutal, Medoc detested Jem in return . . . despised his squeamishness, his attempts to stay clean, his moments of pity when he might have let some small creature go free. According to Medoc he was worse than a lily-livered girl, a snivelling wimp whose pangs of conscience drove Medoc wild. More than once he had drawn a knife and Jem began to fear for his life. What Medoc could do to an animal he could do to him, club him to death and burn his body with the rest. No one would ever know. He was alone in the universe, apart from Medoc. Alone for as long as he could remember.

The ship landed with a thud.

And he coughed nervously.

'What's the matter with you?' growled Medoc.

'Nothing,' said Jem.

'I don't pay sick wages.'

'You haven't paid me anything yet.'

'Don't give me none of your lip, boy! Go and fetch my rifle and let's get started. I want to be away from here by nightfall.'

'Why?' asked Jem.

'Dark,' Medoc said uneasily. 'When the dark comes this is no place to be. Now, get a move on.'

Jem shrugged.

And five minutes later he stood in the hatchway. It seemed an ordinary enough planet, number 506B on the galactic charts. The sun was common yellow and the sky an unspectacular blue, the landscape unremarkable. Temperate grasslands stretched away to rolling forest and snow-capped mountains beyond. Orbital scans suggested an early evolutionary time scale with no advanced life forms, just a few large solitary reptiles and a few herds of warm-blooded animals, most of them relatively harmless. He wondered why it had never been colonized, and even more he wondered why Medoc was afraid.

He watched him stalk through the grasses, a rifle at the ready. Several small cat-like creatures came bounding towards him from the distance. They were delicate and dancing, delightfully alive, with pricked ears and tawny brown fur. Poor little things, thought Jem. Then he shrugged again and went to collect the knives for skinning. He did not particularly want to witness what happened next.

Young, lithe, she leapt through the grasses glittering and shimmering with dew, seeing with each leap the others dancing ahead and the blackened smoking circle of ground that surrounded the ship. It was still far away but the wind carried the scent of it, sharp, acrid, alien, thrilling her senses. She leapt again and saw the hatch-way open, dark, mysterious, a machine giving birth to its beings.

'Star-ones! Star-ones!'

The air was full of welcoming cries and shrill thoughts only she could hear, mind-laughter, joyous and glad-some. She pranced on her hind legs, laughing too, until the shots rang out.

Instinctively she flattened her ears, crouched, hissed, sensing the nearness of some bestial thing, a hunger that was not of her world. And the noise went on, a hideous rattle of sound that hurt inside her head. Above the grasses, silver things streaked in the sun, faster than eye-blinks, metal rain exploding in flesh, terrible and killing. Thought-voices shrieked in sudden agony and bled. Kin-souls screamed, and she felt their death pains in her heart. She did not understand what was happening, but their need was her need and once again she went bounding towards them.

She was one of them, part of them, almost with them, but then she too was struck. Pain burned a pathway through her shoulder, quick and seering. She stumbled and fell, licked the seepage of blood from her fur and whimpered softly. She wanted the others, their caring and comfort, dragged herself forward. But the air was emptying and the first one she found was more hurt than she, its bright eyes dulling with approaching death. She licked its wound, cried softly in her knowing.

'Go!' said its thoughts.

'No,' she whimpered.

'Leave us and save yourself.'

Grasses rustled in the wind and what it said was cruel and unacceptable. It went against all they had ever taught her, all she had ever learned. One alone could not survive. So how could she go? She crawled on to find the next, and the next . . . sister creatures, brother creatures, parent creatures . . . they were all dead or dying, their fading thoughts repeating the same message, telling her to go, run, hide herself in the forest and leave them.

She was all grief, all confusion, and the grasses rustled again. She saw through tears and slender stems a beast bringing in the bodies and another beast, young as she, stripping them of their pelts. For one frozen moment their eyes met, alien blue and slanty yellow. She saw alarm in them, a quick fear that was for her, a kind of warning. He had wild dark hair and his face was pale, bald skin and hairless hands holding a bloodied knife which he jabbed towards her. It was a gesture she understood and her pain was nothing as she turned and fled.

Now she had only one desire. She had to escape. She had to escape the horror of what she had seen, the hideous ugliness, the violation of all her senses. Even the fanged-one was kinder in his killing. It was better to be eaten than brutalized after dying. But there was a shout behind her, a harsh voice crying, and bullets whistled past her ears. She swerved and leapt, sank low among the grass fronds and kept on running, her belly to the earth. Footsteps followed, but still she ran until the sunlight was behind her and the trees closed around with their kind concealing shade. She knew them all and all the forest ways. She knew where to hide herself.

The creature fled.

'Don't just stand there!' snarled Medoc.

'What d'you expect *me* to do?' retorted Jem.

'Go after the bloody thing.'

'Why me?'

'Because I'm in charge of this outfit and you do as you're told. Your legs are younger than mine.'

'Why not let it go?' asked Jem.

'That pelt's worth fifty galactic dollars!'

'Don't you have enough already?'

Medoc turned, his face contorted with fury, snatched the knife from Jem's hand and thrust the rifle in his arms. His voice was savage.

'Get after it, I said! And don't come back without it or I'll nail your hide to a tree! I'm sick of your sodding conscience! Sick of your puking puling namby-pamby tenderness! If you want to see Beldia again you'll bring me that pelt. Nightfall, boy, is all the time you've got. Now beat it!'

Jem stared at him defiantly.

'I hope it gets you,' he said.

'What?' sneered Medoc.

'This planet . . . whatever's on it . . . I hope it gets you!'

Medoc's beard bristled menacingly as Jem backed away. And the knife jabbed viciously towards him, its blade cutting through air, the same gesture Jem had used a minute or so ago. Just as the animal had, Jem understood. He turned on his heel, bitter and hating, and followed it through the grass. There was no point in running. He knew instinctively he had no hope of catching it, nor could he kill it in cold blood on Medoc's say-so, not even to save his own skin. He simply followed it because he had no choice, because there was nothing else he could do, stepping over the dead bodies of its fellows and leaving Medoc behind.

Quietness surrounded him and he felt the sunlight

warm on his back, heard the wind singing through the grasses, the brush of his own steps making a soft rustling sound. The air smelled sweet and clean of dry earth and unknown life, wholesome, invigorating, a relief after months of rottenness, the maggoty stink of Medoc and the ship. Strange birds called in the distances ahead, and the forest seemed almost inviting, the shadows dark beneath its trees. Filled with a sense of freedom Jem walked towards it and he did not look back.

It was better this way, he told himself. Better to stay on the planet than spend another year or two in Medoc's company. He was not worried about how to survive. Brought up in a ghetto in a great sprawling city by a drunken mother and a succession of so-called fathers, he had learnt to fend for himself from an early age and had never relied on people. Relationships were as temporary as places and he had no sense of belonging. This world was as good as any other, he thought. It had a congenial climate, food and water, all that was necessary to sustain a life, and he had a rifle to protect himself. What more did he need?

Nothing, he thought.

'Nothing,' he said aloud.

Insects chirred and white vine flowers trembled, and as he entered the forest the shadows touched him; alien plantlife brooding on its own shade. Tall trees surrounded him and the ground grew soft beneath his feet. He smelled dampness and leafmould, heard the leaves rustle, saw snake-like tendrils and tall ferns swaying. Greenness was everywhere about him. His grip tightened on the gun. He was not fooled by his own logic. Alone, on an unknown planet, he went into exile and he was terribly, horribly, afraid.

Her world had only one law. Things took of life all they needed for their own fulfilment and no more. Even the fanged-one obeyed, killed to satisfy his hunger and knew when he had had enough. But the star-ones had no

177

law. They killed indiscriminately, every one of her kind, and stripped away their pelts. Death without reason . . . the air gone empty of their voices, feeling and thoughts . . . and she alone surviving.

She licked her wound but the pain was not physical. It was somewhere inside her, terrible, unbearable, a soft dark anguish pervading her being. How could she live, alone, in a world with no one to touch or talk with or share her days? A life time bereft of all companionship? One alone was meaningless and she could not even try. It was easier to die, gently, unresisting, there where she lay, not wanting food or drink, unable to care. Dull acceptance absorbed what she felt until nothing remained of her but a tiny inner core of existence, a point of knowingness connecting her external senses to the outside world.

She was part of it still, yet remote and indifferent, uninvolved although she saw and heard and was aware. She was lying on a ledge behind a waterfall, a cool damp hiding place. Clumped ferns surrounded her. Green shade flickered and the air was loud with the rush of the river cascading over the cliff. Through spray and sunlight and rainbows, through a gleaming shimmering moving curtain of water, she gazed with motionless eyes on the forest spread beneath her and the river winding through its valley, its deep pools and shallows and gravelly beaches.

In morning heat she saw a herd of mud-wallowers come to drink. They were grey and hulking, slow moving, witless things, their dung balls feeding the forests on which they fed and their flesh feeding the fanged-one hunting its prey. Already she could sense its presence, see the signs . . . life leaving the river margins, birds fleeing from the thickets, rodents scurrying through the grass, and the mud-wallowers themselves slowly lumbering away.

She watched dispassionately, untouched by emotion, but it was not the fanged-one who came. Wild and pale,

with the death-stick clasped in his arms, the alien
emerged from the jungle into open sunlight. Sweat
beaded his skin and she could smell his fear, see it in his
eyes, flickering blue nervousness. Maybe he knew what
stalked in the still heat beneath the distant trees, and
knew the meaning of the silence. Or maybe he did not
. . . for suddenly he laid the death-stick on the ground
and knelt to drink. Water flowed from his cupped hands
and he seemed oblivious to all else, to the movement
among the leaves and the parting of branches, curved
claws and fangs.

Instinctively she rose to her feet, knowing what would
happen, not choosing to care but caring anyway, shaken
from the deadness of herself. The alien had given her her
life with a gesture and she owed him something.
Ignoring the stiff soreness in her shoulder she left her
hiding place, leapt on to a bare outcrop of rock. And her
warning cries echoed down the valley, her thought-cries
screaming.

'Look out! Look behind you! Run! Run for your life!'

The boy turned his head.

'Run!' she repeated urgently.

Instead he snatched up the death-stick, shot as the
great beast leapt and kept on shooting, blasts of sound
louder than the thunder of falling water, the rattle of
wings. Birds rose in coloured clouds from the jungle,
screaming flocks heading for the foothills of the
mountains. Panicked creatures fled. And in the slow
returning silence the fanged-one lay dead, a great grey
mound on the river's edge, its blood swirling down-
stream. Warily the boy prodded it with his foot and
backed away, then turned suddenly to stare up the
valley, searching for the place the cry had come from,
blue eyes squinting in the light.

Her heart hammered. She was full of feelings she did
not understand, strange little surges of renewed life. She
was hungry, thirsty, but the air smelled of death and
cordite and she did not want to be seen. Quickly she

returned to her hiding place. She was no longer remote or indifferent. Among ferns and shadows, through curtains of shining water, she continued to watch . . . for, strangely, against her will, she had become involved.

Jem shouldered the gun. He was weak and shaking with fear and relief, and something was up there among the high rocks. Sunlight on falling water made him squint and he thought he saw movement, but then he saw nothing. Nevertheless, something or someone was up there, had called out a warning, a cry in the air and words in his head.

He started to climb. The air grew clear and less stifling but it was still hot, the noonday sun beating down on the open slopes; making him sweat with every step. There was no shade anywhere. His head swam and the river boomed in his ears, and his feet kept slipping on loose scree, and low-growing thorny plants scratched him. He headed for the waterfall, needing its coolness, followed what seemed to be a scuffed narrow path among the stones. But it ended in a sheer edge and he could go no further.

It was a good place to rest. He sat on an outcrop of rock with the gun at his feet and surveyed the landscape. Below were deep pools and the river running through its valley, the tract of forest through which he had travelled. It was not very wide. He could see the plain beyond it, an ocean of pale grass rippling in the wind, and on the horizon he thought he could see the ship. It was hard to be sure. It was so far away and small, just a fragment of silver, and the distances behind it were obscured by fog or cloud, a kind of darkness gathering in the sky and on the land, like the first fringes of night. A storm, he thought, and imagined Medoc skinning for all he was worth. He hoped it would rain on him, soak him to his rotten hide and bury him up to his neck in mud. But it would rain on Jem too and in any case he needed to find shelter before nightfall.

He glanced around. Nothing but scree slopes and brooding trees beyond, rugged foothills above him and the river to the left of him plunging over its falls. Then he noticed the ledge. It went across the cliff face behind the curtain of water and might lead to a cave. He could have reached it easily but something was there, guarding the path, a pair of slanty yellow eyes watching him between the fronds of fern.

Fear lurched inside him. He had seen those eyes before, staring at him through the stems of grasses and seeing what he did . . . he, with a skinning knife and blood on his hands, believing he had the right. But he had no right at all. All in an instance he was judged and condemned, damned by his own feelings of guilt and shame and self-disgust, by an animal's eyes, yellow, unblinking, recognizing what he was. He was as bad as Medoc, guilty by association and working for a share of the profits. He bit his lip and looked away, not wanting to remember. They had been bright dancing little cat-like creatures with beautiful tawny fur, alive, and now dead for fifty miserable glactic dollars a piece.

'I'm sorry,' he said without turning his head.

But it was too late for that.

It was too late to apologize.

It was only an animal anyway.

And it would not understand.

'At least *you're* alive,' he told it.

But that was no consolation either.

He still felt bad.

A member of a race of human scum.

And did he really expect an animal to forgive?

Violation against its kind?

Medoc and himself?

He stared bitterly into the distances containing Medoc. The darkness on the horizon was coming nearer, like a cloud or a fog bank creeping across the plain, inky and nebulous, although everywhere around it was bright with afternoon sun. Its slow creeping approach was almost sinister, as if it moved with intention, calculating its path. It made Jem uneasy, filled him with foreboding, and in all his journeying he had seen nothing like it.

He picked up the gun.

'Revenge,' he said.

Then shook his head.

'Don't be stupid, Jem!'

It was only a storm.

But the feeling remained.

And he headed across the scree slopes to the forest.

She could have followed the alien boy but it was too hot for movement; sleepy afternoon when they all dozed in the shade and waited for evening. All were gone and she was alone, unbound by their ways, but she stayed out of habit, sprawled on the ledge behind the waterfall, watching the path in case he returned.

Time moved slowly with the sun. Thirst and hunger troubled her. Yet still she remained, obstinately, refusing to break the tradition of a lifetime, her allegience to her kind. Evening, she thought, come evening she would go and find him, trail his scent among the stones. Unless he had returned to the ship already and would return to the stars?

But no, he was still there, a stranger in a strange world as alone as she was. Across the distance she could feel his presence. He was not just a beast like the fanged-one. He was more like herself, his thought-words betraying a higher consciousness, a regret for his actions that an animal could never know, an awareness of right and wrong. No pity in the fanged-one for its prey, or in the mud-wallowers devastating great tracts of forest. But there had been pity in the alien's eyes, and shame, and sadness too. No animal could judge and condemn itself in that kind of way, so he was not a beast in his knowing. Yet he knew nothing of where he was, her world and all its dangers . . . snake plants and sucker vines and blood flies, poisonous flowers, bad-water pools and hidden quagmires . . . and another thing too.

She rose to her feet, suddenly sensing something she could not remember, out there, in the world, in the sunlight, beyond the horizon and in the dark depths of her mind. She waited a while but the thing and the memory remained elusive, imagined perhaps. She tried to ignore it, but the feeling stayed, a strange unease that made her restless, that grew into agitation and finally drove her out . . . up from the ledge to the high outcrop of rock where the boy's steps ended and began.

She saw it at once, fell mist over the plain, Gorinag, the terrible darkness, the only name she knew. Her hackles rose and her heart missed a beat. Then she was running, ignoring the tearing pain in her shoulder and the fresh welling of blood. Sounds of the waterfall dissolved behind her. Everywhere was still, silent, sunlight beating on stone. But night would come early, and all things hid, and there was silence in the forest, also, when she entered it.

She stopped, listened . . . eerie green shade where not a bird sang, or frog or insect chirred or whistled, where nothing moved among the leaves, or crawled, or crept . . . nothing but a cough somewhere above her, the small crack of a twig, far away footsteps. She turned up hill and headed towards him, speeding on soft paws, soundless in spite of her urgency.

The green heat was stifling but she could feel a chill behind her, fear creeping inexorably nearer, Gorinag searching for a victim, fanged-one or mud-wallower, the alien or herself. She stopped, shuddered, listened again, then changed direction and fled up a familiar trail. It was a path worn over decades by the feet of dead ones and she knew where it led. In company she had travelled it many times before, others laughing and leaping beside her. But now she went alone, and alone she would have to face Gorinag, for there was no one left to help her. No one at all except the boy from the stars. For her own sake as well as his she had to find him.

The trees ended and the land became stony again. A line of sheer cliffs rose before him. Half-way up them Jem saw the dark entrance to a cave. It was what he had hoped to find . . . shelter against the weather, against the night, a perfect place with a single narrow pathway leading up and unapproachable by any other route. Yet he hesitated to climb, afraid of the darkness and what might be inside. Another monster perhaps? Another carnivorous beast like the one he had killed? There were droppings nearby and something must have worn away the forest trail. Nervously he aimed the rifle, fired a series of shots, bullets ricocheting from the rock face, echoing around the hills and down the valley. But the silence returned, louder than before, and nothing moved anywhere, not a bird or an insect or even a blade of grass. It was as if there was nothing left alive beside himself.

The isolation troubled him. He had been alone all his life but never like this, separated from all human kind. And the stillness was intense, almost unnatural, the terrible brooding hush before a storm. The sunlight darkened and the cave waited to swallow him like a black open maw. Jem turned his back on it. First he would eat, he decided. The hunger which so far he had ignored, was growing desperate. He returned to the forest where red fruits grew in clusters from trailing vines. They looked edible but he had no sure way of knowing. Warily, he tasted one, bittersweet but not unpleasant, and better than nothing. He reached for another but, sharp and commanding, the thought-words flashed through his brain.

'Don't eat that! It's poison!'

Jem spat, turned his head.

Small, cat-like, with tawny brown fur, the creature stood where the path emerged a few metres away. There was no one else around, no human person possessed of intelligence and conveying information. Maybe he had imagined the voice and the words? Or maybe he had not.

Maybe other creatures apart from humans were intelligent? He stared at it . . . pricked ears and slanty yellow eyes, recognizing, knowing, staring back at him. Then, slowly and deliberately, needing to test it, Jem put the fruit to his mouth again.

Instantly its cat-eyes narrowed.

Its words hissed through his head.

'It's poison, I tell you!'

Jem threw away the fruit, laughed in delight.

'You!' he said. 'It was you who warned me of the beast!'

'Yes,' said the creature.

'You're not just an animal!'

'Nor are you,' said the creature, 'despite what you've done.'

It was said without accusation, a simple statement of fact, but its truth cut deep. On a scale of moral conduct Jem was pretty low, not much better than Medoc who was the worst kind of scum. He felt vaguely sick, and even more so when the creature moved into the sunlight. There was blood on its pelt, a bullet wound in its shoulder and it limped badly. He bit his lip against the hot flush of shame, a bitter taste in his mouth. But the cat seemed not to care, bore no grudge and showed no fear as it picked its way, delicately, among the tumbled rocks towards him. Its tail flicked in a kind of greeting and, clear and silent, its words came into his head.

'We'll go to the cave,' it said.

'I feel awful,' Jem told it.

'It's the fruit,' it said.

'It's nothing to do with the fruit!'

'You ate it, didn't you?'

'Only one.'

'So, you'll be sick,' declared the cat.

'How sick?'

'Sick enough. But don't worry, I'll look after you.'

'For crying out loud!' said Jem. 'How can you say that?

After what we've done? After what you saw me do? You're making it worse, don't you see?'

'It'll be worse for both of us soon,' said the cat.

'What do you mean?'

'Gorinag's coming.'

'Who's Gorinag?'

'Dark,' said the cat.

'I don't understand.'

'Dark,' it repeated. 'Terrible darkness. We'll go to the cave. Hurry!'

He lay on the floor, in a bed of dried grasses. He had been sick, twice, and his face was grey, his skin clammy to the touch. She gave him water in a gourd cup and tried to rouse him, but apart from the cramps in his stomach he was not aware of very much. And the sun had gone, the plain dissolved into darkness, and inky tendrils of mist were creeping across the forest. She watched from the cave-mouth its slow, silent approach and felt its chill, an icy breathing in the air. Gorinag was cruel and punishing. Things died as it passed and those that survived seldom forgot. She could have fled. There were tunnels at the back of the cave leading deep underground, but she was alone without light, and the boy moaned and writhed and she could neither move him nor leave him, nor wake his mind and make him understand.

She had no choice. Shivering in fear she stood between him and Gorinag, guarding with her life. And the mist came closer, curling like smoke among the trees, as if the whole forest burned with cold black fire. Slowly it covered the land, gathered in clouds at the foot of the cliff, darkening and deepening until it seemed there was nothing left beneath her but pitch-black nothingness. The end of her world was only a step away and if she fell she would fall forever into a bottomless abyss. And the darkness rose to meet her, black freezing destruction. Its night mist touched her in one last moment of terror, coiled about her as she closed her eyes.

It was inescapable and useless to fight it. All she could do was surrender. It was a kind of death, a letting go of all she had ever known and felt, all her grief and loss and loneliness, what she was and had been and wanted to become, all her hopes and fears and joys and pains, the desire to live and the desire to die and even desire itself, until there was nothing left but existence. And then she knew the meaning of Gorinag.

She *was* Gorinag!

She was nothing—everything—the perfect balance of darkness and light, death and life—all was one—she—Gorinag—the universe. Time and seasons turned in her mind. Or maybe she had no mind. She simply existed, as Gorinag existed, almighty unconfined being flowing into all things.

Then there was neither death or darkness. She had gone beyond her own fear into some other state, a bodiless place where only life and light, warm gold and glorious surrounded her. She was this too—energy and power—and the substance of earth and fire and wind and water, stones and stars—the heart of a beast, the essence of a flower, blood on the grass, the scream of a man on an empty plain and the tortured dreams of a boy. What had been done to her world, to her kind, had been done to her too and there could be no pity, although there were tears in her eyes. She wept silently for the loss, and the waste, and the violence . . . wept as the sad, beautiful, terrible, avenging spirit of Gorinag touched her, lingered and moved on.

Then she grew still. She was her own little self again, thinking her own little thoughts. Yet she had learned. She was Gorinag, too, and there was no such thing as death, only the shedding of some old skin. And the air was full of ghosts, full of voices and laughter, kin-souls dancing. All was one and she need never be lonely again. She had only to listen. But the voices faded from her head. She heard the cry of a bird, the distant music of the

187

river and someone in the cave behind her softly, inconsolably crying.

Jem stared at it and felt the horror. It was pale and lifeless, flapping in the wind . . . Medoc's hide nailed to the side of the ship. And his body was meat, piled with the bodies of animals ready for burning. Then it was Jem's turn. Something, or someone he could not quite see, bent over him holding a knife. He supposed he was dead, for his muscles would not obey him. Yet he was aware and still connected by sensation, feeling the first sharp cut, the gush of blood and the slow excruciating peeling away of skin on his forearm. Agony . . . unendurable agony! He screamed, but his screams had no sound.

No pity in the one who skinned and butchered him, no trace of reverence. What was being done stripped him of all humanity. He had only two values . . . meat and money. His hide would be nailed beside Medoc's to dry in the sun and his limbs would be amputated, skewered and spit-roasted over an open fire, or stewed or micro-waved on board the ship. And they came from the darkness and were all around him, ghosts gathering to watch, laughing and jostling, little cats with gleaming yellow eyes and tawny fur. There was nothing he could do. It was too late to apologize, say he was sorry and beg them to forgive. On their behalf something took revenge and he wept helplessly, then suddenly awoke.

It was pitch-dark in the cave.

And there was a creature beside him, warm and nuzzling.

A cat with gleaming yellow eyes.

'No!' sobbed Jem. 'I can't bear it! Not any more!'

Her voice came gently in his mind.

'It's all right. It's over now. Gorinag's gone.'

But the dream remained.

And its contents.

'What about Medoc?' Jem whispered.

'Who?' said the cat.

'The man who was with me?'

'Dead,' said the cat matter-of-factly. 'Dead, I expect. Things do die when Gorinag passes, if they deserve it. Or else they are forgiven.'

'No one can forgive me,' Jem said brokenly.

'Only yourself,' said the cat. 'But Gorinag knew that which is why you survived. I'm glad about that—glad you're with me.'

He sat up, surprised she wished to be associated.

And a spasm of pain gripped his stomach.

'That sodding fruit!'

The small cat laughed as he crawled from the cave, and her laughter reminded him. For as long as he lived he would never forget that dream. And how could she laugh, he wondered, after what had been done to her . . . the wound in her shoulder, her relatives slaughtered? How could she laugh? Maybe she laughed in relief that she was alive and herself, that the air was sweet and a nightbird sang and the moon was brilliant among the stars? But what kind of creature was it that bore no malice, knew no hatred? Not human, Jem thought. She was far finer than any human kind.

He felt strangely humbled, privileged to know her, glad of her company, wanting her to stay. And she was waiting in the mouth of the cave when he returned, a small cat sitting on her haunches, her ears pricked, her yellow eyes gleaming and bright. He wanted to touch her, stroke her tawny brown fur and thank her for being there. Once, thinking she was just an animal, he would have done so, assumed he had a right. But now he was unsure, unsure even if she *was* a she, and with a living thing he would never again take liberties. Whatever she was, whatever sex or species, she was also herself, a creature with her own private thoughts and feelings and a soul that had to be respected.

He squatted on his heels before her.

'What's your name?' he asked.

He saw the puzzlement in her eyes.

'I don't have a name,' she told him.

'Everything has a name.'

She shook her head.

'All is one so there is only one name . . . Gorinag.'

Suddenly Jem understood. He knew what had touched him in the dream and knew what made her as she was. She had no name, no knowledge of herself apart from all other existence, just an awareness of life. And life connected her to everything—to grass and dust and Jem. All was one and she simply loved him as she loved herself and her world.

Tears prickled his eyes. He gazed at the moonlit trees, the undulations of an unknown landscape, an alien planet. It was beautiful and magical and something to be a part of it all. But at the same time he was not a part of it and nor was she. They were both separate, individual beings thinking their own individual thoughts, not even knowing each other. And to express that distinction she needed a name.

'I'll call you Jessa,' he decided.

'Jessa?' she questioned.

'Jessa,' he repeated.

Her eyes were bright.

And she smiled as she watched him.

He did not know she had always longed for the naming of things and her own growing as he wrote her name in the dust.

ABOUT THE AUTHOR

Louise Lawrence lives in Gloucestershire. Her first book, *Andra*, was published in 1971, and since then she has written ten other novels. *Children of the Dust*, published in 1985, won her much acclaim and was shortlisted for both the *Observer* Teenage Fiction Prize and the Library Association's Carnegie Medal. When she is not writing, most of her time is taken up renovating the cottage she shares with her husband.